Financial
ACCOUNTING

CLEP* Test Study Guide

© 2024 Breely Crush Publishing, LLC

*CLEP is a registered trademark of the College Entrance Examination Board which does not endorse this book.

971010221143

Published by Breely Crush Publishing, LLC
10808 River Front Parkway
South Jordan, UT 84095
www.breelycrushpublishing.com

ISBN-10: 1-61433-634-2
ISBN-13: 978-1-61433-634-1

Printed and bound in the United States of America.

Table of Contents

Generally Accepted Accounting Principles

Generally accepted accounting principles (GAAP) are the accounting rules used to prepare financial statements for publicly traded companies. Many private companies also follow GAAP. The accounting standards are not set by the government and GAAP is not written in law. Securities and Exchange Commission (SEC) requires that GAAP be followed in financial reporting by publicly traded companies.

GAAP rules are based with the purpose of achieving the following:

- Financial reporting should provide information that is useful to investors, creditors and other users in making rational investment, credit, and other financial decisions.

- Financial reporting should provide information that is helpful to investors, creditors and other users in assessing the amounts, timing, and uncertainty of prospective cash receipts.

- Financial reporting should provide information that is about economic resources, the claims to those resources, and the changes in them.

In order for the financial statements to be useful and helpful to users, GAAP recommends that financial statements be:

- *Relevant*: Relevant information helps users make predictions about past, present and future events - predictive value. Relevant information helps users confirm or correct prior expectations - feedback value.

- *Reliable*: Reliable information is verifiable, neutral and demonstrates representational faithfulness.

- *Comparable*: Information must be measured and reported in a similar manner for different enterprises so that financial statements can be compared between different companies.

- *Consistent*: The same accounting methods should be applied from period to period so that financial statements of the same company to be compared across periods.

Some of the key assumptions made by GAAP are:

- *Economic Entity Assumption* assumes that the business is separate from its owners or other businesses.

- *Going Concern Assumption* assumes that the business will be in operation for a long time; however, under definite circumstances of liquidation, this assumption is not applicable.

- *Monetary Unit Assumption* assumes a stable currency is going to be the unit of record.
- *Periodic Reporting Assumption* assumes that the business operations can be recorded and separated into different periods.

The SEC has the legal authority to set acceptable accounting methods and looks to the Financial Accounting Standards Board (FASB), a private sector body, for leadership in establishing such standards.

The Financial Accounting Standards Board (FASB) is a private organization which works to create accounting standards which are for the general benefit. Due to the need for comparability and transparency in accounting practices, the SEC requires that all companies adhere to the standards mandated by the FASB. The standard which the FASB created is referred to as GAAP, or Generally Accepted Accounting Principles.

Rules of Double-Entry Accounting

Double-entry accounting system is the standard practice for recording financial transactions. This provides the underlying foundation for a system of accounting, which accumulates and organizes the raw data into useful information. The system is based on the principle that in a business a number of different variables or accounts are used to describe the multiple transactions for a business and each of them has a 'dual effect'.

Dual Effects of Transactions on the Balance Sheet Equation

The balance sheet maintains the equality between the total assets and total liabilities plus total shareholder's equity by reporting the effects of each transaction in a dual manner. Any single transaction will have one of the following four effects or some combination of these four effects:

1. It increases both an asset and a liability or shareholder's equity
2. It decreases both an asset and a liability or shareholder's equity
3. It increases one asset and decreases another asset
4. It increases one liability or shareholder's equity and decreases another liability or shareholder's equity

Examples:

Buying an asset:

1. The amount of fixed assets in the business increases.
2. The amount of cash (also an asset) is reduced.

Selling merchandise on credit:

1. The amount of trade receivables (an asset) for the business increases.
2. The sales revenue for the business increases (eventually becomes part of equity in the form of Retained Earnings).

Paying a creditor:

1. The amount of account payables (a liability) for the business decreases.
2. The amount of cash in the business is reduced.

Prepaid expenses:
It is clear that accounts such as rent and insurance are expenses. This means that they are recorded as an owner's equity account and are increased with a debit. However, sometimes companies will pay expenses in advance – such as paying rent for the whole year in January, or paying insurance a few months ahead. In these cases, the payment actually becomes an asset because it means that there is an expense that the company won't have to pay in the future. These are called prepaid expenses and are recorded as assets. As the expenses arise, the account is adjusted and moved to a regular expense. If prepaid expenses are increased, assets increase. If prepaid expenses are decreased, expenses increase.

T-Account

A balance sheet item can only increase, decrease or remain the same during a period of time. Thus, an account must provide for accumulating the increases and decreases (if any) that occur during the period for a single balance sheet item. The total additions during the period increase the balance carried forward from the previous statement, the total subtraction decrease it, and the result is the new balance for the current balance sheet.

A T-account looks like a letter T with the name or title of the account on the horizontal line.

Account Title

The following rules are used to record transactions:

1. Accounting places increases in assets on the left side and decreases in assets on the right side.
2. Accounting places increases in liabilities on the right side and decreases in liabilities on the left side.
3. Accounting places increases in shareholder's equity on the right side and decreases in shareholder's equity on the left side.

 Debit and Credit

Accountants use two convenient abbreviations – debit (Dr.) and credit (Cr.):

1. *Debit* is used to record an entry on the left side of the account and indicates
   a. Increase in an asset
   b. Decrease in liability
   c. Decrease in shareholder's equity

2. *Credit* is used to record an entry on the right side of the account and indicates
   a. Decrease in an asset
   b. Increase in liability
   c. Increase in shareholder's equity

Accounting Cycle

The accounting process is a series of activities that begins with a transaction and ends with the closing of the books. Since this process is repeated every accounting period, it is called as the accounting cycle. The activities can divided into two broad categories:

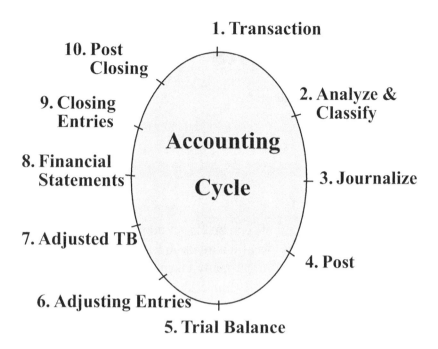

1. Activities that are performed throughout the accounting period
   a. Identify the transaction
   b. Analyze and classify the transaction
   c. Record the transaction using journal entries
   d. Post general entries to the general ledger

2. Activities that are performed at the end of the accounting period
   a. Prepare the trial balance
   b. Prepare adjusting entries to record accrued, deferred and estimated accounts
   c. Post adjusting entries to the ledger and create an adjusted trial balance
   d. Prepare the financial statements (balance sheet, income statement, cash flow statement)
   e. Prepare closing journal entries
   f. Post the closing journal entries to the ledger accounts

🎓 Financial Statements

There are three key financial statements:

1. Balance Sheet
2. Income Statement
3. Cash Flow Statement

The accounts on financial statements can be classified into two different groups – nominal accounts and real accounts. Real accounts are accounts which hold their value from year to year. For example, if a company takes out a loan one year, they will still owe that money the next year. Similarly, the cash in their machines will still be present. Basically any balance sheet account (assets and liabilities) will be a real account. Nominal accounts, on the other hand, have to be closed out at the end of the year. These accounts are measured on a yearly basis. For example, a company would want its sales revenue to accumulate year to year. People are only interested in the current year's sales revenue. This is also true of expenses, gains and losses and dividends. The year end balances of these accounts are transferred to retained earnings.

🎓 Balance Sheet

A *balance sheet* is a snapshot of the investments (assets) of a firm and the financing of those investments (liabilities and shareholder equity) as of a specific time. The balance sheet shows the following balance or equality:

Assets = Liabilities + Shareholder's Equity

This equation states that a firm's assets balance with the financing of those assets by creditors and owners. The sum of liabilities plus shareholder's equity is also referred to as total equity.

A sample balance sheet is shown on the following page:

	2003	2004	2005
Assets			
Cash and Cash Equivalents	$1,798.5	$1,769.2	$1,979.4
Accounts Receivable	113.1	212.3	338.7
Inventories	6.1	14.4	29.3
Total Current Assets	$1,917.8	$1,995.9	$2,347.4
New Build Property & Equipment, net	1,493.3	2,693.3	4,360.0
Acquired Property & Equipment, net	1,866.7	1,733.3	1,600.0
Franchise Rights	900.0	750.0	550.0
Goodwill	0.0	0.0	0.0
Other Assets	40.7	152.9	243.9
Total Assets	$6,218.5	$7,325.5	$9,101.3
Liabilities & Stockholders' Equity			
Notes Payable to Bank	$0.0	$0.0	$0.0
Current Portion of Long-Term Debt	264.7	418.5	641.7
Current Portion of Capital Leases	0.0	0.0	0.0
Accounts Payable	30.7	72.2	146.7
Other Liabilities	40.7	152.9	243.9
Total Current Liabilities	$336.1	$643.6	$1,032.3
Long-Term Debt	$2,530.6	$3,148.2	$3,983.3
Capital Leases	0.0	0.0	0.0
Franchise Fees	514.3	428.6	342.9
Other Liabilities	40.7	152.9	243.9
Total Liabilities	$3,421.7	$4,373.3	$5,602.4
Shareholders' Equity			
Common Stock	$3,500.0	$3,500.0	$3,500.0
Retained Earnings	(703.2)	(547.8)	(1.1)
Total Liabilities & SE	$6,218.5	$7,325.5	$9,101.3

Asset Recognition

An asset is a resource that has the potential for providing a firm with a future economic benefit – the ability to generate future cash inflows or to reduce future cash outflows. A firm will recognize a resource as an assets only if

1. the firm has acquired rights to its use in the future as a result of a past transaction or exchange

2. the firm can measure or quantify the future benefits with a reasonable degree of precision

 # Asset Valuation

There are several methods that are used to assign a monetary amount to each asset in the balance sheet.

1. *Acquisition or Historical Cost:* The amount of cash paid (or the cash equivalent of other forms of payment) in acquiring an asset is referred to as the acquisition or historical cost of the asset.

2. *Current Replacement Cost:* This represents the amount *currently* required to acquire, or enter into, the rights to receive future benefits from the asset.

3. *Current Net Realizable Value:* The net amount of cash (selling price less selling costs) that a firm would receive *currently* if it sold each asset separately, is referred to as the current net realizable value or the exit value.

4. *Present Value of Future Net Cash Flows:* This is today's value of a stream of *future* cash flows.

Useful Tip: If the asset value is measured through future cash flows, you should discount the future cash flows to determine the present value as of the date of the balance sheet!

GAAP Accepted Asset Valuation Basis

The financial statements currently prepared by publicly held firms use two valuation bases for assets that have not significantly declined in value since the firm acquired them. These are:

1. *Monetary Assets* such as cash and accounts receivable generally appear on the balance sheet at their net present value – their current cash or cash equivalent value.

2. *Non-monetary Assets* such as merchandise inventory, land, buildings and equipment generally appear at acquisition cost, in some cases adjusted downward to reflect the assets' services that have been consumed and to recognize some declines in market value.

 # Asset Classification

The classification of assets within the balance sheet varies widely in published annual reports. Some of the principal categories are:

1. *Current Assets:* Cash and other assets that a firm expects to realize in cash or to sell or consume during the normal operating cycle of the business are referred to as current assets.

   Example: cash, marketable securities held for the short term, accounts and notes receivable, inventories of merchandise, raw materials, supplies, work in progress, finished goods and prepaid operating costs.

2. *Investments:* This includes long-term (non-current) investments in securities of other firms.

3. *Property, Plant and Equipment*: This (also called fixed assets) represents the tangible, long-lived assets used in a firm's operations over a period of years and generally not acquired for resale. The balance sheet shows these items (except land) at acquisition cost reduced by the cumulative depreciation since the firm acquired the assets. Frequently, only the net balance or book value appears on the balance sheet.

   Example: land, buildings, machinery, automobiles, furniture, fixtures, computers and other equipment.

4. *Intangible Assets*: Such items as patents, trademarks, franchises and goodwill are intangible assets. Accountants generally do not recognize as assets those expen-

ditures that a firm makes in developing intangibles because of the difficulty in ascertaining the existence and value of future benefits. Accountants do however, recognize as assets those specifically identifiable intangibles that firms acquire in market exchanges from other entities – intangibles such as a patent acquired from its holder.

Shareholder's Equity Valuation and Disclosure

The shareholder's equity in a firm is residual interest – that is the owners have a claim on all assets not required to meet the claims of the creditors. The valuation of the assets and liabilities included in the balance sheet therefore determines the valuation of total shareholder's equity.

Accounting distinguished between capital contributed by owners and earnings retained by the firm. The balance sheet for a corporation generally separates the amount that the shareholder's contribute directly for an interest in the firm (or common stock) from earnings the firm subsequently realizes in excess of dividends declared (or retained earnings).

In addition, the balance sheet also further disaggregates the amount received from shareholders into the *par* or *stated* value of the shares and the amounts contributed in excess of par value or stated value (or additional paid-in capital).

Overview of the Accounting Process

The double-entry framework records the results of various transactions and events in the accounts to enable the periodic preparation of financial statements. The accounting system designed around the recording framework generally involves the following operations:

1. Entering the results of each transaction in a book called the *general journal* in the form of a *journal entry* – a process called *journalizing*

2. Copying the amount from the journal entries in the general journal to the accounts in the general ledger – a process called *posting*

3. Preparing a *trial balance* of the accounts in the general ledger

4. Making adjusting and correcting journal entries to the accounts listed in the trial balance and posting them to the appropriate general ledger accounts

5. Preparing financial statements from a trial balance after adjusting and correcting entries

 # Income Statement

The *income statement* provides a measure of the operating performance of a firm for some particular period of time.

Net Income (or earnings) = Revenue – Expenses

Revenues measure the net assets (assets less liabilities) that flow into a firm when it sells goods or renders services.

Expenses measure the net assets that a firm consumes in the process of generating revenues.

A sample income statement is shown below:

	2003	2004	2005
Sales	$1,357.0	$5,096.3	$8,128.8
Cost of Goods Sold	315.5	1,169.8	1,849.0
Gross Profit	$1,041.5	$3,926.5	$6,279.8
Operating Expenses:			
Restaurant Operating Expenses	$398.3	$1,621.8	$2,554.3
Franchise Royalties	80.1	300.7	479.6
Franchise Fee	100.0	150.0	200.0
Advertising Fee	67.9	254.8	406.4
Rent - Stores	262.5	378.5	557.0
Rent - Office	30.0	30.9	31.8
General and Administrative	358.9	398.0	627.0
EBITDA	($256.1)	$791.8	$1,423.6

Depreciation & Amortization	240.0	333.3	466.7
EBIT	($496.1)	$458.5	$956.9
Interest Expense	$260.1	$338.8	$447.7
Interest Income	$53.0	$35.7	$37.5
Pre-Tax Profit	**($703.2)**	**$155.4**	**$546.7**
Taxes	0.0	0.0	0.0
Net Income	**($703.2)**	**$155.4**	**$546.7**

 # Presentation Format Issues with the Income Statement

Financial statement users study a firm's income statement to analyze its past and future profitability. When assessing profitability, the analyst tries to determine the following regarding the nature of income items:

1. Does the income result from a firm's primary operating activity or from an activity that is peripheral to the primary operating activity?

2. Does the income result from an activity the firm will continue its involvement in or the income was from an unusual transaction and the event is unlikely to occur regularly?

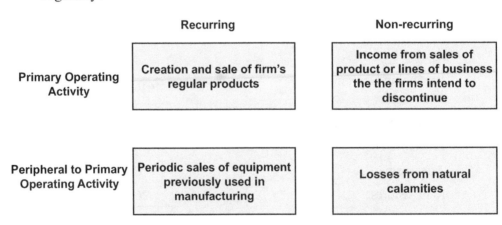

A financial statement user who is interested in evaluating a firm's ongoing operations will focus on the items in the upper left corner while one who is interested in projecting net income of prior periods into the future would focus on the recurring income cells as income items in the non-recurring cells should not affect ongoing assessments of profitability.

A key distinction needs to be made between gain vs. income and loss vs. expense. Revenues and expense result from the recurring, primary operating activities of a business whereas gains and losses occur from the either the peripheral activities or nonrecurring activities. Another key distinction is that while gains and losses are net concepts, income and expenses are gross concepts. As an example, a toy manufacturer is selling its computers that were used for data processing and are now obsolete. The computers originally cost $200,000 and have an accumulated depreciation of $150,000. The company sells the computers for $80,000 and thus records a gain of $30,000 over the book value of $50,000. The journal entry for such a transaction would be as below:

Cash..80,000		
Accumulated Depreciation.....................................150,000		
Equipment...200,000		
Gain on sale of equipment...30,000		

Note that the income statement reports only the gain from sale and not the selling price. The income statement reports only the gain and loss as financial statement users do not need information on the components of either the peripheral or the nonrecurring income items.

Accounting for Irregular Items

(Such as Discontinued Operations and Extraordinary Items)

Income statements contain the following sections:

1. *Earnings from continuing operations*: Revenues, gains, expenses and losses from the continuing areas of business activity of a firm appear in the first section of the income statement. This section includes both the earnings derived from a firm's primary business activities as well as from activities peripherally related to operations. The key point to note is that the firm expects these sources of earnings to continue.

2. *Earnings, gains and losses from discontinued operations*: This section includes any earnings, gains and losses related to the sale of any discontinued operation. Firms typically report these earnings, gain or loss on a single line net of income tax effects. This is reported in a separate section so that it is clear that this income is not a recurring source of income.

3. *Extraordinary gains and losses*: This section reports extraordinary gains and losses. For an item to be extraordinary, it must generally meet both the following conditions:

  • Unusual in nature

  • Infrequent in source

4. *Adjustments for changes in accounting principles*: If a firm changes its methods of accounting during a period, the firm must disclose the effects that the changes had on net earnings of current and previous years.

Profitability Analysis

This section discusses the three widely used measures of profitability:

1. Rate of return on assets
2. Rate of return on shareholders equity
3. Earnings per share of common stock

RATE OF RETURN ON ASSETS

An indicator of how profitable a company is relative to its total assets. ROA gives an idea as to how efficient management is at using its assets to generate earnings. Calculated by dividing a company's annual earnings by its total assets, ROA is displayed as a percentage. Sometimes this is referred to as "return on investment".

Note: Some investors add interest expense back into net income when performing this calculation because they'd like to use operating returns before cost of borrowing.

ROA tells you what earnings were generated from invested capital (assets). ROA for public companies can vary substantially and will be highly dependent on the industry. This is why when using ROA as a comparative measure, it is best to compare it against a company's previous ROA numbers or the ROA of a similar company.

The assets of the company are comprised of both debt and equity. Both of these types of financing are used to fund the operations of the company. The ROA figure gives investors an idea of how effectively the company is converting the money it has to invest into net income. The higher the ROA number, the better, because the company is earning more money on less investment. For example, if one company has a net income of $1 million and total assets of $5 million, its ROA is 20%; however, if another company earns the same amount but has total assets of $10 million, it has an ROA of 10%. Based on this example, the first company is better at converting its investment into profit.

RATE OF RETURN ON SHAREHOLDERS EQUITY

Return on common equity - earnings before extraordinary items, less preferred-share dividends, divided by average common shareholders' equity. ROE shows the rate of return on the investment for the company's common shareholders, the only providers of capital who do not have a fixed return.

$$ROE = \frac{Net\ income}{Sales} \cdot \frac{Sales}{Total\ Assets} \cdot \frac{Total\ Assets}{Average\ stockholders\ equity}$$
$$= \frac{Net\ income}{Average\ stockholders\ equity}$$

(profit margin times total asset turnover times financial leverage, DuPont ratio)

ROE can be seen as a measure of how well a company used reinvested earnings to generate additional earnings, equal to a fiscal year's after-tax income (after preferred stock dividends but before common stock dividends) divided by total equity, expressed as a percentage.

EARNINGS PER SHARE

Earnings per share (EPS) are the earnings returned on the initial investment amount. The FASB requires companies' income statements to report EPS for each of the major categories of the income statement: continuing operations, discontinued operations, extraordinary items, and net income.

The EPS formula does not include preferred dividends for categories outside of continuing operations and net income. This formula also shows the most basic formula for earnings per share.

$$Earnings\ Per\ Share = \frac{Income}{Weighted\ Average\ Common\ Shares}$$

The EPS formula is shown here for Net Income and Continuing Operations (substitute income from continuing operations for net income).

$$\text{Earnings Per Share} = \frac{\text{Net Income-Preferred Dividend}}{\text{Weighted Average Common Shares}}$$

Earnings per share for continuing operations and net income are more complicated in that any preferred dividends are removed from net income before calculating EPS. Remember that preferred stock rights have precedence over common stock. If preferred dividends total $100,000, then that is money not available to distribute to each share of common stock.

The value used for company earnings can either be the last twelve months' net income (referred to as trailing-twelve-months), or analysts' predictions for the next twelve months' net income (referred to as forward). The number of shares used for the calculation can either be basic (only shares that are currently outstanding) or diluted (includes all shares that could potentially enter the market).

Companies often use a weighted average of shares outstanding over the reporting term. (The weight refers to the time period covered by each share level) EPS can be calculated for the previous year ("trailing EPS"), for the current year ("current EPS"), or for the coming year ("forward EPS"). Note that last year's EPS would be actual, while current year and forward year EPS would be estimates.

 Acquisition and Disposal of Long-Term Assets

ACQUISITION OF ASSETS

The cost of a plant asset includes all charges necessary to prepare it for rendering services. The cost of a piece of equipment will be the sum of the entries to recognize the invoice price less discounts, transportation costs, installation charges and any other costs incurred before the equipment is ready for use.

When a firm constructs its own buildings or equipment, it will record many entries in these asset accounts for the labor, material and overhead costs. GAAP requires the firm to capitalize interest paid during construction as part of the cost of the asset being constructed. The total amount of interest capitalized cannot exceed total interest costs for the period. The capitalization of interest into plant assets reduces otherwise reportable interest expense and thus increases income. However, this will be compensated in the future when the plant shows depreciation expense, reducing income.

IMPAIRMENT OF ASSETS

A firm acquires assets for their future benefits. Accounting does not permit assets whose values have declined substantially to remain on the balance sheet at amortized acquisition cost. If the current book value exceeds the sum of expected undiscounted cash flows, asset impairment has occurred and the firm is expected to write down the book value of the asset to its then current fair value.

RETIREMENT OF ASSETS

At the time of retiring an asset, before making the entry to write off the asset and its accumulated depreciation, the firm records an entry to bring the depreciation up to date. That is, the firm records the depreciation that has occurred between the start of the accounting period and the date of the disposition. When a firm retires an asset from service, it removes the cost of the asset and the related amount of accumulated depreciation from the books. As part of this entry, the firm records the amount received from the sale, a debit and the amount of net book value removed from the books, a net credit. The excess of the proceeds received on the retirement over the book value is gain or a loss.

As an example, consider a firm decides to retire equipment whose cost is $50,000, has an expected life of four years and a salvage value of $2,000. The firm has recorded an annual depreciation of $12,000 for two years and is selling the equipment at the end of the second year. The equipment has a book value of $26,000 and the firm is selling the equipment for $20,000. The journal entries will be as follows:

Cash...20,000	
Accumulated Depreciation.......................................24,000	
Loss on Retirement of Equipment...............................6,000	
Equipment..50,000	

The loss on retirement recognizes that the past depreciation charges have been too small and appears on the income statement and reduces retained earnings.

🎓 Amortization

Intangible assets such as patents, copyrights, trademarks are all reflected in a company's financial records. There are two ways that they can be amortized. If a company creates a patent or copyright themselves then its value is recorded as simply the small cost incurred in obtaining it. If a patent or copyright is purchased from another company then its value is recorded as the purchase amount. Because these intangible assets have a limited useful life (patents and copyrights both expire) they are amortized over time, generally using the straight line method of accounting. This means that over time the value of the asset is reduced to reflect its current value. For example, if a patent is purchased for $100,000 and has a useful life of five years then each year $20,000 of amortization expense would be recorded (the full journal entry being a $20,000 debit to amortization expense and a $20,000 credit to accumulated amortization).

The expenses are initially added to the value of the asset, and transferred from the balance sheet to the income statement using a fixed schedule, usually a constant amount per accounting period.

The proper use of amortization allows the organization to properly recognize that such expenses contribute to productivity or profitability over a relatively long period. The determination of which intangible assets can be amortized and what period to use can have significant effects on the apparent profitability of an enterprise, and consequently can affect the stock price of a publicly traded corporation. GAAP require all intangible assets acquired after 1970 to be amortized over a period no longer than 40 years.

The corresponding concept for tangible assets is termed depreciation.

🎓 Depletion

In addition to plant assets, companies also own natural resources called *wasting assets*. Depletion refers to the amortization of these wasting assets. Accounting capitalizes in an asset account the costs of finding natural resources and of preparing to extract them from the earth. GAAP allows two treatments:

1. *Full Costing* capitalizes the cost of all explorations – whether successful or not – so long as the expected benefits from the successful explorations will more than cover the cost of all explorations.

2. *Successful Efforts Costing* capitalizes the costs of only the successful efforts. The cost of unsuccessful exploration becomes expenses of the period when the fact becomes apparent that the efforts will not result in productive sites.

Most of the firms use units of production depletion method. As an example, ABC Inc. incurs $6 million in costs to discover an oil field that contains estimated 2 million barrels of oil. This firm would amortize the cost of $6 million at $3 ($6 million/2 million) for each barrel of oil removed from the field.

Intangible Assets such as Patents and Goodwill

PATENTS

A patent is a right granted by the federal government to exclude others from the benefits of an invention. Legal life of patent protection can extend for 20 years although it may have a short economic life. The accounting for patent costs depends upon whether the firm purchased the patent from another party or developed it internally. If the firm purchased the patent, it capitalizes the costs. If the firm developed the patent internally, it expenses the total costs of product development as required by all R&D costs. FASB has not given reasoning to justify this distinction in accounting treatment of purchased versus developed patents. The firm will amortize the cost of purchased patent over a period equal to the shorter of remaining legal life or its estimated economic life. If for some reason the patent suffers impairment in value, the firm treats it like other long lived but impaired asset.

GOODWILL

Goodwill can arise when one company purchases another company or operating unit from another company. The acquiring firm must put each of the acquired assets and liabilities onto its balance sheet at the fair market value of the items acquired on the date of acquisition. The acquired asset, such as a patent or a trademark developed earlier by the acquired firm will appear on the balance sheet even though it may not appear on the balance sheet of the firm being acquired.

Accounting measures goodwill as the difference between the amount paid for the acquired company as a whole and the sum of the current values of its identifiable net assets. In computing goodwill, the acquiring company compares the purchase price to the sum of the fair values of the individual assets less the sum of the fair values of the individual liabilities even if those assets and liabilities do not appear on the acquired company's balance sheet. Goodwill appears on the balance sheet of the company making the acquisition.

Example: On January 1, 2006, XYZ Inc. acquires ABC Inc. whose book value of the shareholder's equity is $100 million and the market value of shareholder's equity is $300 million. XYZ Inc. amortizes goodwill over 20 years.

	ABC Inc.	**XYZ Inc.**
Cash	$25,000.00	$ 25,000.00
Inventories	$40,000.00	$ 47,500.00
PP&E	$60,000.00	$ 75,000.00
Patents developed		$ 80,000.00
Patents purchased	$45,000.00	$ 48,500.00
Brand Names		$ 55,000.00
Current Liabilities	$30,000.00	$ 30,000.00
Long-term debt	$50,000.00	$ 57,000.00

What will be the new asset and liability valuations on the XYZ Inc. balance sheet if it paid $350 million to acquire ABC Inc? What will be the annual charge for amortization of goodwill?

Solution: The assets and liabilities of ABC Inc. will also appear on the balance sheet of XYZ Inc. In addition, new asset goodwill in the amount of $50 million ($350 million - $300 million) will also appear on the balance sheet of XYZ Inc. Goodwill will be amortized at $50 million/20 = $2.5 million per year.

Owner's Equity

Accountants disclose the common shareholder's equity of a firm in various accounts on the balance sheet:

Capital Contributions: Shares of common stock usually have either a par or stated value specified by the articles of incorporation and appears on the face of the certificate. The par value of the stock has little economic substance and the issue price of a share depends on its market value. Receipts from the issuance of common stock that exceed the par value are recorded as *Additional Paid-in Capital*.

Earnings and Dividends: The assets that a firm generates from earnings in excess of amounts payable to creditors and preferred shareholders belong to the common shareholders. Net income allocable to the common shareholders there increases the *retained earnings* account each period and when the dividends are distributed the retained earnings account is reduced.

Accumulated Other Comprehensive Income: Even though some operating transactions affect the economic value of a firm, they do not affect net income or retained earnings until a future period. Firms include such items in Accumulated Other Comprehensive Income, a component of shareholder's equity distinct from capital contributions and retained earnings. Accumulated Other Comprehensive Income includes unrealized gains or losses from investments in securities held for sale.

Treasury Share Transactions: Firms sometimes reacquire shares of their outstanding common stock for various corporate purposes. Such reacquired shares are called as Treasury shares and since they reduce the owner's claims on the firm's assets, they appear as a subtraction from total shareholder's equity.

So technically, when a company looks at shareholders' equity (or specifically the statement of shareholders' equity), they can learn several things: how much was left over (positive or negative in value) last year, what is the difference in revenues and expenses experienced by the company (net income or net loss) of the year at hand, and how much was paid out in dividends in the year at hand.

Preferred Stock

A preferred stock is a share of stock carrying additional rights above and beyond those conferred by common stock. Unlike common stock, preferred stock usually has several rights attached to it.

- Preferred stock owners get preference in dividends. Before a dividend can be declared on the common shares, any dividend obligation to the preferred shares must be satisfied.

- The dividend rights are cumulative, such that if the dividend is not paid it accumulates in arrears.

- Preferred stock has a par value or liquidation value associated with it. This represents the amount of capital that was contributed to the corporation when the shares were first issued.

- Preferred stock has a claim on liquidation proceeds of a stock corporation, equivalent to its par or liquidation value unlike common stock, which has only a residual claim.

- Almost all preferred shares have a fixed dividend amount. The dividend is usually specified as a percentage of the par value or as a fixed amount.

- Some preferred shares have special voting rights to approve certain extraordinary events (such as the issuance of new shares or the approval of the acquisition of the company) or to elect directors, but most preferred shares provide no voting rights associated with them.

- Usually preferred shares contain protective provisions which prevent the issuance of new preferred shares with a senior claim. This results in corporations often having several series of preferred shares that have a subordinate relationship.

Preferred shares are more common in private companies, where it is more useful to distinguish between the control of and the economic interest in the company. Also, government regulations and the rules of stock exchanges discourage the issuance of publicly traded preferred shares.

There are various types of preferred stocks that are common to many corporations:

- *Cumulative Preferred Stock* - This type of stock is almost like a corporate bond in the sense that the company is obliged to pay the dividend if it makes a profit. In the case of a loss, the dividend will accumulate and has to be paid in future years.

- *Non-cumulative Preferred Stock* - Dividend for this type of preferred stock will not accumulate if it is unpaid.

- *Convertible Preferred Stock* - This type of preferred stock carries the option to convert into a common stock at a prescribed price.

Common Stock

Common stock or common shares, are the most usual and commonly held form of stock in a corporation. Common stock that has been re-purchased by the corporation is known as treasury stock and is available for a variety of corporate uses.

Common stock typically has voting rights in corporate decision matters, though perhaps different rights from preferred stock. In order of priority in a liquidation of a corporation, the owners of common stock are near the last. Dividends paid to the stockholders must be paid to preferred shares before being paid to common stock shareholders.

Retained Earnings

In accounting, retained earnings or retained profits are profits that have not been paid to a company's shareholders as dividends.

They are reported in the ownership equity section of a firm's balance sheet. A complete presentation of the companies retained earnings position is presented in the statement of retained earnings.

The decision of whether a firm should retain profits or disburse them as dividends depends on several factors including: the firm's judgment of its own investment opportunities relative to those available in the market and any difference in tax treatment of dividends paid now and capital gains expected to result from investing retained earnings.

Liquidity, Solvency, & Activity Analysis

Market liquidity is a business or economics term that refers to the ability to quickly buy or sell a particular item without causing a significant movement in the price. The essential characteristic of a liquid market is that there are ready and willing buyers and sellers at all times. An elegant definition of liquidity is also the probability that the next trade is executed at a price equal to the last one.

Liquidity risk can be both short-term as well as long-term. The measures for assessing the short-term liquidity risk are:

Current Ratio

The current ratio is a comparison of a firm's current assets to its current liabilities. For example, if ABC Inc.'s current assets are $10 million and its current liabilities are $8 million then its current ratio would be $10 million divided by $8 million which equals 1.25.

The current ratio is an indication of a firm's market liquidity and ability to meet short-term debt obligations. Acceptable current ratios vary from industry to industry, but a current ratio between 1 and 1.5 is considered standard. If a company's current assets are in this range, then it is generally considered to have good short-term financial strength. If current liabilities exceed current assets (the current ratio is below 1), then the company may have problems meeting its short-term obligations. If the current ratio is too high, then the company may not be efficiently utilizing its current assets.

Quick Ratio

One measure that is used in financial analysis to determine the liquidity of a company is called the current ratio. The current ratio is a measure of a company's ability to meet its short run obligations. The formula for the current ratio is Current Assets / Current Liabilities. Current assets are defined as assets which are easily converted to cash, or are already in cash form. Examples of current assets are cash and cash equivalents, accounts receivable and inventory. Liabilities are considered current liabilities if they must be paid within the current fiscal year. Examples of current liabilities include short term loans payable, accounts payable, unearned revenue, taxes payable and interest payable.

The Acid-test or quick ratio measures the ability of a company to use its "near cash" or quick assets to immediately extinguish its current liabilities. Quick assets include those current assets that presumably can be quickly converted to cash at close to their book values. Such items are cash, stock investments, and accounts receivable. This ratio implies a liquidation approach and does not recognize the revolving nature of current assets and liabilities. It compares a company's cash and short-term investments to the financial liabilities the company is expected to incur within a year's time.

Ideally the acid test ratio will be 1:1, but 0.8:1 is acceptable, any less and the business could suffer financial difficulties.

Cash flow from Operations to Current Liabilities Ratio

Some analysts are not in favor of using the current ratio or the quick ratio as they use amounts at a specific time and if financial statement amounts at that time are unusually large or small, the resulting ratios may not provide accurate information. The Cash flow from Operations to Current Liabilities Ratio overcomes these problems. The numerator for this ratio is the cash flow from operations for that year and the denominator is the average of current liabilities. A health firm normally has a ratio of 40% or more.

Analysts use measures of long-term liquidity risk to evaluate a firm's ability to meet interest and principal payments on long-term debt and similar obligations. A firm's ability to generate profits over several years provides the best protection against long-term liquidity risk. The measures for assessing the long-term liquidity risk are:

Debt Ratio
The debt to equity ratio (D/E) is a financial ratio, which is equal to an entity's total liabilities divided by shareholders' equity. The two components are often taken from the firm's balance sheet (or statement of financial position), but they might also be calculated using their market values if both the company's debt and equity are publicly traded. It is used to calculate a company's "financial leverage" and indicates what proportion of equity and debt the company is using to finance its assets.

Interest Coverage Ratio
This ratio is calculated by dividing a firm's earnings before interest and taxes (EBIT) of one period by the company's interest expenses of the same period. The lower the ratio the more the company is burdened by debt. When a company's interest coverage ratio is 1.5 or lower, its ability to meet interest expenses may be questionable. An interest coverage ratio below 1 indicates the company is not generating sufficient revenues to satisfy interest expenses.

Cash Basis of Accounting

Under the *cash basis of accounting*, a firm recognizes revenues from selling goods and services in the period when it receives cash from customers. It reports expenses in the period when it makes cash expenditures for merchandise, salaries, insurance, taxes and similar items.

The cash basis does not adequately match the cost of the efforts required in generating revenues with those revenues. The performance of one period mingles with the performance of preceding and succeeding periods. The longer the period over which a firm receives future benefits, the more deficient the cash basis for reporting becomes.

Another problem with the cash basis of accounting is that it postpones the time when the firm recognizes the revenue.

Accrual Basis of Accounting

The accrual basis of accounting recognizes the revenue when the firm sells goods or renders services. The costs of assets used in producing revenues lead to expenses in the period when the firm recognizes the revenues that the costs helped produce. Thus, accrual basis of accounting matches expenses with associated revenues and is the preferred method for most of the firms.

Timing of Revenue Recognition

The accrual basis of accounting recognizes revenue when both of the following events have occurred:

1. A firm has performed all, or most of, the services it expects to provide
2. The firm has received cash or some other asset capable of reasonably precise measurement such as a receivable

Timing of Expense Recognition

Accountants recognize expenses as follows:

1. If asset expiration associates directly with a particular revenue, that expiration becomes an expense in the period when the firm recognizes the revenue. This treatment – the *matching principle* – matches cost expirations with revenues.
2. If asset expiration does not clearly associate with revenues, that expiration becomes an expense of the period when the firm consumes the benefits of the asset in operation.

Relation Between Balance Sheet and Income Statement

The balance sheet and the income statement are related by the following equation:

Net Income = Retained Earnings – Retained Earnings + Dividends
(end of period) (beginning of period)

After preparing the income statement at the end of the period, the balances in the income and expense accounts are transferred to the Retained Earnings account. The Retained Earnings account measures the cumulative excess of earnings over dividends since the firm began its operations.

Adjusting Entries

Adjusting entries prepared at the end of the accounting period change the balances in the general ledger accounts so that revenue and expense accounts reflect correct amounts for measuring net income for the period and assets, liabilities and shareholder's equity accounts report correct amounts for measuring financial position at the end of the period.

Recognition of Accrued Revenues / Receivables and Accrued Expenses / Payables:
A firm earns revenues as it renders services. However, recording these amounts as they accrue day by day is not convenient. Hence, an adjusting entry is made at the end of the period to account for the earned revenue as an asset on the balance sheet and as revenue on the income statement.

Similarly the firm might have received some services and goods for which the expense might not have been recording resulting in the need of an adjusting entry.

Allocation of Prepaid Operating Costs:
Another type of adjustment arises because a firm acquires assets for use in operations but does not completely use them during the accounting period when acquired. The portion of the used asset should be adjusted as an expense and the asset reduced by the same amount in the balance sheet.

Recognition of Depreciation:

When a firm purchases assets it debits their acquisition cost to appropriate asset accounts. Although these assets may provide services for a number of years, their future benefits expire as time passes. Accounting spreads an asset's cost over the periods of the asset's estimated useful life. The term *depreciation* refers to the charge made to the current operations for the portion of the cost of such assets consumed during the current period.

The most widely used method, the straight-line method, allocates an equal portion of the acquisition cost, less estimated salvage value, to each period of the assets estimated useful life. The straight-line depreciation method computes depreciation charge for each period as follows:

$$\frac{\text{Acquisition Cost - Estimated Salvage Value}}{\text{Number of periods in Estimated Useful Life}} = \text{Depreciation charge for each period}$$

Note that depreciation expense (an income statement account) includes depreciation for the current accounting period only, whereas accumulated depreciation (a balance sheet account) includes the cumulative depreciation charges since the firm acquired the assets.

 # Trial Balance after Adjusting Entries

The accountant posts the adjusting entries in the general ledger in the same manner as entries made during the period. After making the adjusting entries, the accountant prepares a trial balance of the general ledger accounts. This *adjusted trial balance* helps in preparing the financial statements.

 # Preparing the Income Statement

The adjusted trial balance shows all revenue and expense accounts with their correct amounts for the period. This can be used to prepare the income statement by listing all the revenue accounts, listing all the expense accounts, and showing the difference between the sum of the revenues and sum of the expenses as *net income*.

Revenues and expenses related to the firm's principal business activity appear in a separate section that results in reporting the amount of *operating income* for the year. Revenues and expenses related only peripherally to operations, usually investing and financial activities, appear in a separate section. Income taxes appear in a third section. Multiple subtractions result in various sub-totals before arriving at net income.

Closing of Temporary Accounts

Revenue and expense accounts are temporary labels for portions of retained earnings. Once the adjusted trial balance is prepared, the revenue and expense accounts have served their purpose for the current period and the accounting process closes these accounts. The former debit (credit) balances in temporary accounts become debits (credits) in the retained earning account.

Statement of Cash Flows

A *cash flow statement* classifies the reasons for the change in cash as an operating, investing or financing activity. A sample Cash Flow statement is shown below:

	2003	2004	2005
Operating Activities			
Net Income	($703.2)	$155.4	$546.7
Plus: Depreciation and Amortization	240.0	333.3	466.7
Decr. (Incr.) in Accounts Receivable	(113.1)	(99.3)	(126.4)
Decr. (Incr.) in Inventories	(6.1)	(8.3)	(14.9)
Decr. (Incr.) in Other Assets	(940.7)	37.8	109.0
Incr. (Decr.) in Accounts Payable	30.7	41.5	74.5
Incr. (Decr.) in Other Liabilities – ST	40.7	112.2	91.0
Incr. (Decr.) in Other Liabilities – LT	555.0	26.5	5.3
Cash from Operating Activities	($896.8)	$599.2	$1,152.0
Investing Activities			
Capital Expenditures	(1,600.0)	(1,400.0)	(2,000.0)
Acquisitions	(2,000.0)	0.0	0.0
Cash from Investing Activities	($3,600.0)	($1,400.0)	($2,000.0)

Financing Activities

Increase/(Decrease) of Debt	$2,795.3	$771.5	$1,058.3
Increase/(Decrease) of Equity	0.0	0.0	0.0
Cash from Financing Activities	$2,795.3	$771.5	$1,058.3
Net Change in Cash	($1,701.5)	($29.4)	$210.2
Cash @ BOY	0.0	1,798.5	1,769.2
Cash @ EOY	$1,798.5	$1,769.2	$1,979.4

Cash flow from operations indicates the extent to which the operating activities have generated more cash then they have used.

Cash flow from investing activities indicates the cash used in the acquisition of non-operating assets.

Cash flow from financing activities indicates the cash obtained from short and long term borrowing, from issues of common or preferred stock or the cash paid out to pay dividends, repay short and long term borrowings and to reacquire shares of outstanding common or preferred stock.

The effect of net income on cash change equation is as follows:

Change in cash = change in liabilities + change in shareholders equity – change in net current assets

Valuation of Accounts and Notes Receivable

The figure below shows the operating activities for a typical manufacturing firm.

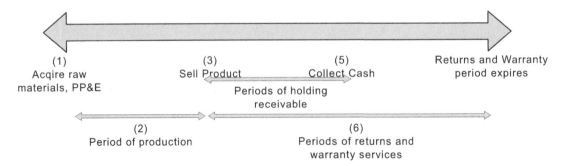

The operating activities of some firms satisfy the revenue recognition criteria during (2) while others might not meet the criteria till they receive cash from customers (5) and some (eg: those dealing with untested products) might not be able to recognize till the end of (6). Recognizing revenue at the time of sale and properly matching expenses with revenues requires firms to estimate the cost of uncollectible accounts, returns and recognize them as expenses at the time of sale. In this section, we discuss the valuation of accounts and notes receivable, estimation of uncollectible accounts and income recognition at times different from sale.

Accounts receivable typically arises when a firm sells goods or services on account. The journal entry is as below:

Accounts Receivable..250		
Sales Revenue..250		

Receivables may arise from transactions other than sales. For example, a firm may give advances to officers or employees or make deposits to guarantee performance or cover potential damages.

One measure that can be important for a company to understand is their accounts receivable turnover. This ratio is the measure of how long it takes for them to collect the money from sales on credit. The accounts receivable turnover is determined using the formula Net Credit Sales/Average Accounts Receivable. Because not all companies record net credit sales (they just record sales revenue as a whole, including both cash and credit) sometimes sales revenue must be used. Also, if only one set of data is available, accounts receivable can be used without averaging it to other values. Although these substitutions make the value less accurate, it is often necessary. The result of the calculation is the number of times in a year that accounts receivable is turned over – in other words, how many times it is filled and emptied (therefore, how often they collect the money from their sales).

Occasionally in accounting there are accounts which are directly correlated to each other in which one account is meant to offset the other. For example, reflected on the balance sheet of many companies is machinery and the depreciation of the machinery. Depreciation is recorded under the asset heading so that it can be easily identified, however it actually has the effect of reducing it. Because of this, depreciation is considered a contra asset account and has a normal credit balance. Other contra assets include allowance for bad debt and depletion expense. Another example of a contra account is the contra revenue account of sales returns and allowances. Although this account is listed with sales revenue it has the effect of reducing it and will have a normal debit balance.

Uncollectible Accounts

Whenever a firm extends credit to customers, it will almost certainly never collect from some of their customers. The principle accounting issue related to uncollected accounts concerns when firms should recognize the loss from uncollectible accounts.

Direct Write-Off Method

The direct write-off method recognizes losses from uncollectible accounts in the period when the firm decides that specific customer's accounts are uncollectible. The journal entry is as below:

Bad Debt Expense...250

Accounts Receivable 250

This method has the following three drawbacks:

1. It does not usually recognize the loss in the period in which the sale occurs and the firm recognizes the revenue.
2. It provides the firm with an opportunity to manipulate earnings each period by deciding when particular customers' accounts become uncollectible.
3. The amount of accounts receivable on the balance sheet does not reflect the amount a firm expects to collect in cash.

Firms must use this method for income tax reporting whereas GAAP does not allow the firms to use this method when they have significant amounts of uncollectible accounts which can be reasonably predicted (eg: retail stores).

Allowance Method

When a firm can estimate with reasonable precision the amount of uncollectible accounts, this is the preferred GAAP method. It involves the following two steps:

1. Estimate the net amount of the receivables the firm expects to collect.

2. Adjust the balance sheet amount of accounts receivable, with an entry to a balance sheet contra account, to reflect that expected net amount. Typically, the adjustment involves a credit to the asset contra account. Match this credit with a debit to the Bad Debt Expense or Provision for Uncollectible account.

Bad Debt Expense...250

Allowance for Uncollectible Accounts 250

When a firm judges particular accounts to be uncollectible, it writes off the account and debits the Allowance for Uncollectible Accounts.

Allowance for Uncollectible Accounts..................................250

Accounts Receivable 250

The allowance method requires firms to estimate the amount of uncollectible before the time when actual uncollectible accounts occur which provides the management an opportunity to manipulate earnings which may not become evident for several accounting periods. Thus, quality-of-earnings issues arise under both the direct write-off and the allowance method.

One of the most common methods to estimate the amount of uncollectible accounts is the *Percentage-of-Sales Method*. This is based on multiplying the total sales account by a pre-determined percentage - usually between ¼% to 2% of credit sales - to estimate the uncollectible account.

 # Income Recognition Before the Sale

Firms sometimes recognize revenue and expense before the sale of a product at time (2).

Percentage-of-Completion Method

The percentage-of-completion method recognizes a portion of the contract price as revenue or expense depending upon the proportion of total work performed. For example, assume that firm is constructing a condo for $400,000 and estimates that the total cost would be $320,000 which would occur as follows: Year 1, $80,000; Year 2, $160,000; Year 3, $80,000. For this firm, the revenue and expense would be recorded as below:

Year	Degree of Completion	Revenue	Expense
1	$80,000/$320,000=25%	$100,000	$80,000
2	$160,000/$320,000=50%	$200,000	$160,000
3	$80,000/$320,000=25%	$100,000	$80,000

 # Completed Contract Method

Some firms postpone revenue recognition (even though the might have completed parts of the project) until they have completed the entire project. For such a firm, there would be no revenue or expense recognition in years 1 and 2 for the above example. The firm would recognize revenue of $400,000 and an expense of $320,000 in year 3.

 # Income Recognition After the Sale

The operating process for some firms requires substantial performance after the time of sale. For other firms, it involves considerable uncertainty regarding the future amounts of cash inflows, cash outflows or both. In these cases recognizing income after the time of sale – (4), (5) or (6) is appropriate.

 # Installment Method

This recognizes revenue as the seller collects parts of the selling price in cash. In parallel, this recognizes as expenses each period the same portion of the COGS as the portion of the total revenue recognized. For example, assume a firm sells a product for $80 which costs it $60. The buyer agrees to pay $20 each month (ignoring the interest). So, the firm would recognize revenue of $20 and expense of $15 every month for four months.

Cost-Recovery-First Method

When the seller has substantial uncertainty about the amount of cash it will collect, it can use this method which matches the costs of generating revenues dollar for dollar with cash receipts until the seller recovers all costs. Using the example above, the seller would recognize revenue and expense of $20 for the first three months and revenue of $20 in the fourth month.

GAAP allows the use of these methods only when the seller cannot make reasonably certain estimates of cash collection.

Valuation of Inventories

The term *inventory* means a stock of goods or other items that a firm owns and holds for sale or for further processing as part of ordinary business operations. Accountants must allocate the total cost of goods available for sale during a period between the current period's use (COGS, an expense now) and the amounts carried forward to future periods (end-of-period entry, an asset now but an expense in the future)

Beginning Inventory + Additions - Withdrawals = Ending Inventory
        (goods available for use or sale)

Example: A firm has a beginning inventory of $500 and an ending inventory of $400. During the year, inventory worth $150 was purchased. What is the COGS?

Solution: COGS is the same as withdrawals in the inventory equation,

$$500 + 150 - COGS \text{ (Withdrawals)} = 400$$

Therefore, COGS = $250

Cost Basis for Inventory

The basis for valuing inventory – the rule for assigning a cost to a physical unit – affects the periodic net income as well as the mount at which the inventories appear on the balance sheet. Some of the methods used are:

Acquisition Cost Basis values units in inventory at their historical cost until sold.

Current Cost Basis values units in inventory at a current market price:

- *Replacement Cost* is the amount the firm would have to pay to acquire the item at that time.
- *Net Realizable Value* is the amount that a firm would realize as a willing seller in an arms-length transaction with a willing buyer.

Lower-of-Cost or Market Basis is the smaller of the two amounts – acquisition cost or market value (measured as replacement cost) and is the preferred method by GAAP.

Standard Cost is predetermined estimate of what items of manufactured inventory should cost.

Specific Identification and the Need for a Cost Flow Assumption

If a firm has more goods available for sale than it uses or sells, and if it finds specific identification not feasible or desirable, it must make some assumptions about the flow of costs. The accountant computes the acquisition cost applicable to the units sold and to the units remaining in the inventory using one of the following cost flow assumptions:

1. *First-in, first out (FIFO)* cost flow assumptions assigns the costs of the earliest units acquired to the withdrawals and assigns the cost of the most recent acquisitions to the ending inventory. This cost flow assumes that the firm uses the oldest materials and goods first.

   For example: A DVD player manufacturer has three identical items in stock as below:

Item	Date of Purchase	Cost
Item 1	1-Jan-05	$100
Item 2	1-Feb-05	$120
Item 3	1-Oct-05	$140

The selling price of the final product is $200. What is the COGS, ending inventory, sales and gross margin for this company if it sells only one player in the year? Assume FIFO.

Sales = $200

COGS = $100 (since item 1 was purchased the earliest)

Ending Inventory = $120+$140 = $260

Gross Margin = Sales – COGS = $100

2. *Last-in, first out (LIFO)* cost flow assumptions assigns the costs of the latest units acquired to the withdrawals and assigns the cost of oldest acquisitions to the ending inventory. Some analysts believe that since LIFO matches current costs to current revenues; it is a better measure for income.

Using the example above, for LIFO:

Sales = $200

COGS = $140 (since item 3 was purchased the latest)

Ending Inventory = $100+$120 = $220

Gross Margin = Sales – COGS = $60

3. *Weighted Average* cost flow assumption calculates the average of the cost of all goods available for sale. The weighted average cost applies to the units sold during the period and to units on hand at the end of the period.

Using the example above, for weighted average:

Sales = $200

COGS = $120 ((100+120+140)/3 =120)

Ending Inventory = $240 ($120*2 = $240)

Gross Margin = Sales – COGS = $80

Of the three cost flow assumptions, FIFO results in balance sheet figures that are the closes to the current cost because the latest purchases dominate the ending inventory amounts. The COGS expense tends to be out of date and when purchase prices rise,

FIFO usually leads to reporting of a higher net income and when prices fall, it results in a lower net income.

LIFO ending inventory contains costs of items acquired long time back and thus when purchase prices rise, LIFO usually leads to reporting of a lower net income and when prices fall, it results in a higher net income. LIFO's COGS figure closely represents current costs.

Weighted average cost flow assumption falls in between FIFO and LIFO but it resembles FIFO more than LIFO in its impact on the financial statements.

 LIFO Layers

In any year when purchases exceed sales, the quantity of units in inventory increases. The amount added to inventory for that year is called a *LIFO layer*. A firm using LIFO must worry about dipping into LIFO layers as it reduces current taxes in periods of rising purchase prices and rising inventory quantities. LIFO can induce firms to manage LIFO layers and COGS in a way that would be unwise in the absence of tax effects. LIFO also gives the management the opportunity to manipulate income: under LIFO, end-of-year purchases, which the firm can manipulate, affect net income for the year.

Initial Costs of Plant and Assets

The cost of a plant asset includes all charges necessary to prepare it for the rendering services. The cost of a piece of an equipment will be the sum of the entries to recognize the invoice price (less any discounts), transportation costs, installation charges and any other costs incurred before the equipment is ready for use.

When a firm constructs its own building or equipment, it will record many entries in these asset accounts for the labor, material and overhead costs incurred, GAAP require the firm to include (capitalize) interest paid during construction as part of the cost of the asset being constructed. The inclusion of the interest stops after the firm has finished constructing the asset.

Depreciation

The firm can keep most plant assets intact and in usable operation condition for more than a year but will eventually retire them from service (with exception of land). Depreciation systematically allocates the cost of these assets to the periods of their use.

Depreciation is a process of cost allocation and is not a process of valuation. Over the entire service life of a plant asset, the asset's value declines from acquisition until the firm retires it from service. The charge made to the operations of each accounting period does not measure the decline in value during that period but rather represents a process of cost allocation – a systematic process, but one in which the firm has some freedom to choose. If, in a given period, an asset increases in value, the firm will still record depreciation during that period, there have been two partially offsetting processes:

- A holding gain on the asset which historical cost-based accounting does not recognize.
- An allocation of the asset's historical cost to the period of benefit which accounting does recognize.

The three principal accounting issues in allocating the cost of an asset over time are as follows:

1. measuring the depreciable basis of the asset
2. estimating the useful service life
3. deciding on the pattern of expiration of asset cost over the useful service life

Depreciable Value of Plant Assets

Since residual value is what the firm receives at the end of the useful life of the asset, it is not depreciated.

Estimating Salvage Value

The terms salvage value and net residual value refers to estimated proceeds on the disposition of an asset less all removal and selling costs.

For buildings, common practice assume salvage value to be zero since it is assumed that the cost to be incurred in tearing down the building will approximate the sales value of the material required (salvage value). Internal Revenue Service provides that a firm may ignore salvage value entirely in calculating depreciation for tax reporting.

Unit of Account

Whenever feasible, a firm should compute depreciation for individual items such as a single building, machine or automobile. When the firm uses many similar items each one with relatively a small cost, individual calculations become impracticable and the firm computes the depreciation charge for the group as a whole.

Estimating Service Life

The depreciation calculation requires an estimate of the economic service life or depreciable life of the asset. In making the estimate, the accountant should consider both the physical as well as the functional causes of depreciation.

Since obsolescence typically results from forces outside the firm, accountants have difficult anticipating obsolescence well enough for them to be reasonably confident of their estimate. For this reason, accountants reconsider assets' estimated service lives every few years. Income tax laws allow a firm to use a life shorter than estimated service life in computing depreciation for tax reporting, but the firm must use the estimated service life and not the shorter tax life for financial reporting.

Pattern of Expiration of Costs

The figure below shows some of the most common methods used for computing the depreciation of an asset

I: No depreciation

II: Straight line depreciation

III: Accelerated depreciation

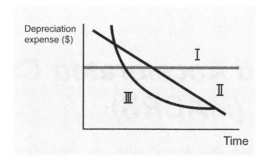

Straight Line Method

Financial reporting most commonly uses the straight-line method which divides the cost of the asset less any estimated salvage value by the number of years its expected life.

$$\text{Annual depreciation} = \frac{\text{Cost less estimated salvage value}}{\text{Estimated life in years}}$$

Example: A machine costs $20,000 and has an estimated life of 10 years. If the salvage value is $5,000, what is the annual depreciation?

Annual depreciation = ($20,000 - $5,000)/10 = $1,500

Accelerated Method

This method allows faster write-offs than allowed by the straight line method. These methods provide a greater tax shield effect than straight line depreciation, and so companies with large tax burdens prefer to use accelerated depreciation methods, even if it reduces the income shown on financial statement. Accelerated depreciation methods are popular for writing-off equipment that might be replaced before the end of its useful life since the equipment might be obsolete (e.g. computers).

Some of the most common methods used for accelerated depreciation of an asset are:

1. Modified Accelerated Cost Recovery System (MACRS)
2. Declining-Balance Methods

 # Modified Accelerated Cost Recovery System (MACRS)

In declining-balance depreciation, each period's depreciation is based on the previous year's net book value, the estimated useful life, and a factor.

$$Depreciation\ expense = Previous\ period's\ NBV \times \frac{factor}{N}$$

 # Declining-Balance Methods

For the double-declining balance method, the factor is commonly two; this is known as double declining-balance. Each period we calculate depreciation:

$$Previous\ period's\ NBV \times \frac{factor}{N} = \$17000 \times \frac{2}{5} = \$16800$$

The figure below shows the relationship between the accumulated depreciation and net book value of an asset.

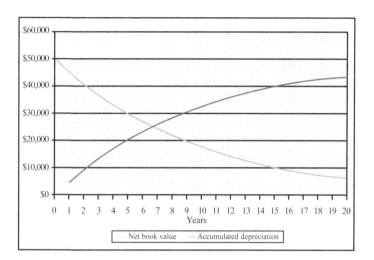

Reporting of Depreciation on the Financial Statements

Firms generally disclose the asset's cost and accumulated depreciation on the balance sheet in one of the following three ways:

1. All information is listed in the balance sheet

Property Plant and Equipment	
Acquisition Cost	250
Less Accumulated Depreciation	(150)
Property Plant and Equipment (net)	100

2. Acquisition cost is omitted from the balance sheet

Property Plant and Equipment, less	250
Accumulated Depreciation of $150	100

3. Acquisition cost and accumulated depreciation are omitted from the balance sheet and are detailed in the notes

---

Property Plant and Equipment (net)..100

Depreciation expense appears in the income statement sometimes disclosed separately an sometimes as part of COGS expense.

Liabilities

The balance sheet typically classifies liabilities in the following categories:

1. *Current Liabilities:* Obligations that a firm expects to pay or discharge during the normal operating cycle of the firm, usually one year, are referred to as current liabilities.

2. *Long-Term Debt:* Obligations having due dates or maturities more than one year after the balance sheet date are long-term debts.

3. *Other Long-Term Liabilities:* Obligations not properly considered as current liabilities or long-term debt appear as other long-term liabilities, which include such items as deferred income taxes and some retirement obligations.

Liability Recognition

A liability arises when a firm receives benefits or services and in exchange promises to pay the provider of those goods or services a reasonably definite amount at a reasonably definite future time. All liabilities are obligations but not all obligations are accounting liabilities.

Liability Valuation

Just like assets, liabilities can be either monetary or non-monetary.

1. *Monetary Liabilities:* These liabilities require payments of specific amounts of cash. Those due within one year or less appear at the amount of cash the firm

expects to pay to discharge the obligation. If the payment dates extend more than one year into the future, the liability appears at the present value of the future cash flows.

2. *Non-monetary Liabilities:* A liability that requires delivering goods or rendering services rather than paying cash is non-monetary.

Long-Term Liabilities

The long term liabilities include mortgages, bonds, notes and leases. Borrowers usually pay interest on long term liabilities at regular intervals during the life of a long term obligation whereas they pay interest on short term debt in a lump sum at maturity.

When the borrower makes a cash payment, a portion of the payment represents interest and any excess of cash payment over interest expense reduces the borrower's liability for the principal amount. Long term debt can be retired in several ways but the accounting is the same for all. In the next section, accounting for retirement of a bond is illustrated under different scenarios.

 Bonds

The price at which a firm issues bonds on the market depends on two factors: the future cash payments that the bond indenture requires the firm to make and the discount rate that the market deems appropriate given the risk of the borrower. The issuing price equals the present value of the required cash flows discounted at the appropriate market interest rate.

Accounting for bonds issued at more than par
Suppose a 5-year bond with a par value of $100,000 and 12 percent interest is issued for $107,721

Cash...107,721	
Bonds Payable...107,721	

The total interest paid over the life of the bond is $60,000 and the effective interest per month is $60,000 - $7,721 = $52,279. In the first month, the interest paid is 5% of $107,721 = $5,386 and the coupon payment is $6,000.

Interest Expense 5,386	
Bonds Payable 614	
Interest Payable	6,000

Investments

For a variety of reasons, companies often acquire the marketable securities (bonds and other stocks) of other companies. Relatively short-term holdings of corporate securities usually appear as *marketable securities* in the current assets section of the balance sheet. The accounting of investments depends upon the purpose of this investment and on the percentage of voting stock that one corporation owns of another. The figure below shows the different types of investments and the GAAP suggested guidelines for ownership.

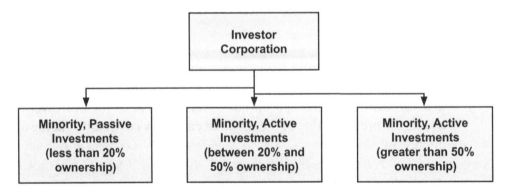

Valuation of Securities at Acquisition

A firm initially records the acquisition of securities at acquisition cost which includes the purchase price plus any commissions, taxes and other costs incurred.

Marketable Securities...250	
Cash..	250

Dividends on equity securities become revenue when declared. Interest on debt securities become revenue when earned. Example: Assume that a firm holds equity securities earning $150 through dividend declarations and debt securities earning $200 from interest earned and that it has to yet receive these amounts in cash.

Dividends and Interest Receivable 350	
Dividend Revenue...	150
Interest Revenue...	200

Valuation of Securities After Acquisition

The accounting for marketable securities available for sale involves three transactions or events:

1. Acquisition of Marketable Securities

Marketable Securities...	Acquisition Cost
Cash..	Acquisition Cost

2. Reevaluation to market value at the end of the accounting period

Marketable Securities...	Increase in market value above book value
Unrealized holding gain on securities available for sale	Increase in market value above book value
Unrealized holding loss on securities available for sale	Decrease in market value below book value
Marketable Securities...	Decrease in market value below book value

3. Sale of Marketable Securities

Securities sold for amount larger than acquisition cost

Cash...Proceeds of Sale
      Marketable Securities...Acquisition Cost
      Realized gain on sale of securities ....Plug amount

Securities sold for amount smaller than acquisition cost

Cash...Proceeds of Sale
Realized loss on sale of securities... Plug amount
      Marketable Securities...Acquisition Cost

The realized loss or gain accounts appear in the income statement before closing to Retained Earnings. Once the firm has sold the securities, it no longer has an unrealized gain or loss from these securities. The final step in the accounting eliminates from the balance sheet the recording of the unrealized holding gain or loss.

Unrealized holding gain on securities............................. Excess of book value above
 available for sale   acquisition cost

Marketable Securities... Excess of book value above
                                                        acquisition cost

---

FASB *Statement No. 115* requires the following disclosures each period:

1. The aggregate market value, gross unrealized holding gains, gross unrealized holding losses and amortized cost for debt securities held to maturity and debt and equity securities available for sale.

2. The proceeds from sales of securities available for sale and the gross realized gains and the gross realized losses on those sales.

3. The change during the period in the net unrealized holding gain or loss on securities available for sale included in a separate shareholder's equity account.

4. The change during the period in the net unrealized holding gain or loss on trading securities included in earnings.

Trading securities are securities and investments which were purchased with the intent of resale in a short period of time. However, unlike most assets, trading securities are reflected at their current market value, not at their historical cost. This is done by evaluating the value of the securities each time the balance sheet is redone.

Consolidated Statements

When one firm, P, owns more than 50 percent of the voting stock of another company such as S, P can control the activities of S. Common usage refers to the majority investor as the *parent* and to the majority owned company as the *subsidiary*. GAAP require the parent to combine the financial statements of majority-owned companies with those of the parent in *consolidated financial statements*.

Cash and Stock Dividends

A firm may choose to pay dividends in the form of cash, other assets or shares of its common stock.

Cash Dividends

Once a dividend has been declared, it becomes a legal liability of the firm and entry is as below:

Retained earnings	100,000
Dividends Payable	100,000

Once the dividend is paid, the entry is as below:

Dividends Payable	100,000
Cash	100,000

Stock Dividends

The key point to remember is that a stock dividend has no effect to the shareholder's equity as it reallocates amount from retained earnings account to contributed capital account. GAAP requires the firms to record the value of the newly issued shares based on the market value of the shares issued. Assume a stock dividend of $100,000 is issued using 5,000 stocks at a market value of $20 and a par value of $10.

Retained Earnings	100,000
Common Stock ($10 par)	50,000
Additional Paid-in Capital	50,000

Treasury Stock

Companies sometimes buy back their shares for a variety of reasons. In most cases, it is a sign management believes the stock is undervalued. Depending upon its objectives, a company can either retire the shares it purchases, or hold them with the intension of reselling them to raise cash when the stock price rises.

This action reduces the amount of shareholder's equity and increases the proportion of debt in the capital structure making the firm more risky and making it less attractive to an unfriendly buyer.

Accounting for Treasury Shares

Accounting for treasury shares follows from the same fundamental principle that a corporation does not report profit or loss on transactions involving its own shares. Accounting views treasury share purchases and sales as capital not operating transactions and therefore debits ("loss") or credits ("gain") the contributed capital accounts for the adjustments for reissue of treasury shares.

When a firm reacquires common shares, it debits a treasury shares – common account (a shareholder's equity contra account) with the total amount paid to reacquire the shares.

Treasury Shares - common		250
Cash		250

If the firm later reissues treasury shares for cash, it debits ash with amount received and credits the treasury shares – common account with the cost of the shares.

Cash		350
Treasury Shares - common		250
Additional Paid-in capital		100

Division of Profits and Losses in Partnership Accounting

A partnership is defined as the relationship that exists between persons carrying on a business. These persons agree to combine some or all of their property, labor, and skills and the business relationship is based on a mutually agreeable contract.

Each partner must use a capital and a withdrawals account to record changes in their financial positions. They must allocate for division of profits and/or losses amongst themselves.

There are three methods of dividing earnings. They can be divided on a stated fractional basis, divided according to the ratio of capital investment, or they can be divided through the use of salary and interest allowances.

Stated Fractional Basis

Each partner receives a fraction of the total. Example: Two partners A & B agree to split earnings on a fractional basis where A gets 1/5 and B gets 4/5. Total earnings were $80,000.

A would get 1/5 * $80,000 = $16,000, B would get 4/5 * $80,000 = $64,000

Ratio of Capital Investments

Under this scenario, the earnings are divided according to the amount each partner has invested. For example: A invested $20,000; B $40,000. The total amount invested is $60,000.

Therefore, A invested $20,000/$60,000 or 1/3 of the total capital and B invested $40,000/$60,000 or 2/3 of the total capital.

Therefore, A would get 1/3 of the total earnings, while B would get 2/3.

 # Salary and Interest Allowances

Using this method, partners may be given part of the earnings as salary and/or interest. Generally, the interest payments are percentages based on their capital investments. The remaining earnings are divided according to an aforementioned fixed ratio.

 # Managerial Accounting

Management accounting is concerned with the provisions and use of accounting information to managers within organizations, to assist management making decisions and managerial control functions. Unlike financial accountancy information (which, for the most part, is public information), management accounting information is used within an organization and is usually confidential.

An operating budget is the annual budget of an activity stated in terms of Budget functional/sub-functional categories and cost accounts. It contains estimates of the total value of resources required for the performance of the operation including reimbursable work or services for others. It also includes estimates of workload in terms of total work units identified by cost accounts.

Full cost accounting generally refers to the process of collecting and presenting information (costs as well as advantages) for each proposed alternative when a decision is necessary. Costs and advantages may be considered in terms of environmental, economical and social impacts. Full cost accounting information may be used by decision-makers. Full cost accounting embodies several key concepts that distinguish it from standard accounting techniques. The following list highlights the basic tenets of FCA.

- Accounting for costs rather than outlays
- Accounting for hidden costs and externalities
- Accounting for overhead and indirect costs
- Accounting for past and future outlays
- Accounting for costs according to lifecycle of the product

Some of the tools used in managerial accounting to determine the costs of producing a good include breakeven analysis, direct costing and absorption costing.

Cost-Volume Profit (Breakeven Analysis)

Break-even analysis helps determine the level of sales necessary to operate a business on a break-even basis. At break-even, total costs (fixed costs plus variable costs) equals' total revenue, i.e., there is neither a profit nor a loss. If you produce more units than at the break-even level, you will be generating a profit. On the other hand, if you produce less than the break-even level, you will be losing money.

Some of the common terns used in performing a break-even analysis include:

- Selling Price (SP): This is the price that each unit will sell for. This is expressed in dollars per unit.

- Variable Cost (VC): These consist of costs that vary in proportion to sales levels. They can include direct material and labor costs, the variable part of manufacturing overhead, and transportation and sales commission expenses. VC is expressed in dollars per unit.

- Contribution Margin (CM): This is equal to sales revenues less variable costs or SP - VC.

- Fixed Costs (FC): These costs remain constant within the projected range of sales levels. FC includes facilities costs, certain general and administrative costs, and interest and depreciation expenses. FC is expressed as a lump-sum cost in dollars.

The number of units sold at break-even is:

No. of Units at breakeven = FC / (SP - VC)
Break-even revenue ($) = (Break-even units) x (Selling Price)

Example: John Doe Inc. manufactures widgets. Each unit retails at $1.5. It costs John Doe Inc. $1 to make each one, and the fixed costs for the period are $300. What is the break-even point in units and in sales revenue?

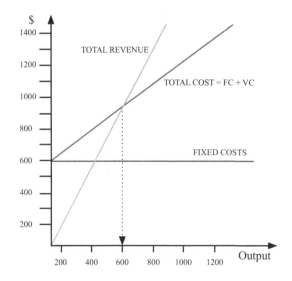

SP = $1.5
VC = $1.00
FC = $300.00

Break-even units
 X = FC / (SP - VC)
 = $300 / ($1.5 - $1)
 = $300 / $0.5
 = 600 units

Break even sales revenue = break-even units x SP
 = 600 x $1.5
 = $900

Direct Costing and Absorbing Costing

Direct costing method includes only the variable manufacturing costs. This is also known as the *variable costing* or *marginal costing* method. These costs are expenses in the year in which they occur.

The costs included are:

- *Direct materials:* those materials that are an integral part of the finished product and can be directly related to it
- *Direct labor:* those labor costs that can be directly attributed to the manufacturing of the finished product
- *Overhead:* only variable manufacturing overheads are factored

Absorption costing also known as *full cost method* is a costing method that includes all manufacturing costs (direct materials, direct labor), variable and fixed overhead in unit product costs. Using an absorption costing system, the profit reported for a manufacturing business for a period will be influenced by the level of production as well as by the level of sales. This is because of the absorption of fixed manufacturing overheads into the value of work-in-progress and finished goods stocks.

Net income when costs are classified by function for absorption costing is calculated as below:

Gross Margin = Sales - Cost of goods sold (Manufacturing costs)
Net Income = Gross margin – Selling and administrative expenses

Net income when direct costing is used is calculated as below:

Contribution Margin = Sales - Variable expenses
Net Income = Contribution margin - Fixed expenses

The key difference in profit calculations using absorption costing and direct costing is as below:

- If beginning and ending inventory are the same, absorption costing profit = direct costing profit
- If ending inventory is lower than beginning inventory, direct costing profit > absorption costing profit
- If ending inventory is higher than beginning inventory, direct costing profit < absorption costing profit

Financial Statement Analysis

Financial analysis is the analysis of the accounts and the economic prospects of a firm. Such an analysis has the objective to assess the firm's:

- performance, for the management to improve it,
- solvency, so as for a bank or a supplier to grant a credit,
- potential value to decide an investment or divestment. Then it is called fundamental analysis and is linked to business valuation and stock valuation.

Financial analysts, among other tasks, use to compare financial ratios (of solvency, profitability, growth...)

- between several periods (the last 5 years for example)
- between similar firms

Those ratios are calculated by dividing a (group of) account balance(s), taken from the balance sheet and / or the income statement, by another, for example:

Net profit / equity = return on equity
Gross profit / balance sheet total = return on assets
Stock price / earnings per share = P/E-ratio

Performance Evaluation

There are several metrics that can be used to measure the performance of an organization. Some of the key metrics include:

RETURN ON INVESTMENT (ROI)

Return on investment (ROI), is calculated as follows:

ROI = Operating income/Average operating assets

Operating assets are assets used to generate operating income like - cash, working capital, inventory, PP&E etc.

Average Operating Assets = (Beginning net book value + Ending net book value)/2

ROI encourages managers to focus on the relationship among sales, expenses, and investment and also provides incentive to improve operating asset and cost efficiency. However, it can also result in myopic behavior with the managers focusing on the short run at the expense of the long run. For example, a manager might cut research and development expenses in the short run to improve ROI, but the cuts may not be in the best long-term interests of the division.

In addition, it also discourages managers from investing in projects that would decrease the ROI of their project/department but would increase the profitability of the company as a whole which is not good for the firm as a whole.

ECONOMIC VALUE ADDED (EVA)

This is a performance measure calculated as after-tax operating profit minus the total annual cost of capital.

EVA = After-tax operating income – (actual percentage cost of capital × Total capital employed)

Total capital employed includes:

- amount paid for buildings, land, and machinery
- other expenditures meant to have a long-term payoff, such as research and development and employee training

A positive EVA indicates that the company earned operating profit greater than the cost of the capital used and is creating wealth. EVA encourages the management to consider the cost of capital when making decisions.

BALANCED SCORECARD

The balanced scorecard is a strategic responsibility accounting system that translates an organization's mission and strategy into operational objectives and performance measures for four different perspectives:

1. *Financial perspective* - describes the economic consequences of actions taken in the other three perspectives
2. *Customer perspective* - defines the customer and market segments in which the business operates
3. *Internal business process perspective* - describes the internal processes needed to provide value for customers and owners
4. *Learning and growth perspective* - defines the capabilities that an organization needs to create long-term growth and improvement

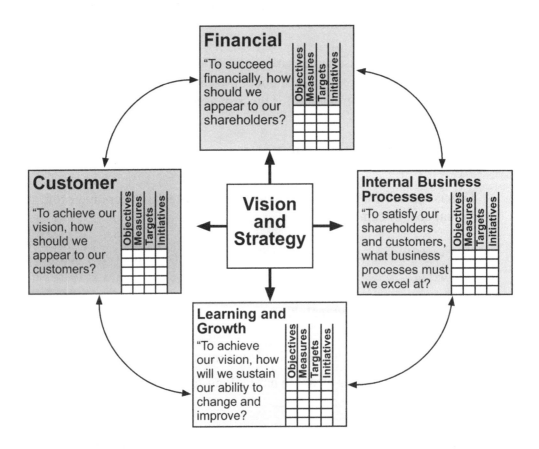

Process and Job Order Systems

There are two types of costing systems used in manufacturing and service companies:

1. Process costing
2. Job-order costing

Process Costing

This system is used in companies which produce a single, homogeneous product or service. In this system, total manufacturing costs are divided by total number of units produced during a given period. Process costing is used in industries such as cement, flour, brick, and oil refining.

 # *Job-Order Costing*

This system is used when different types of products, jobs, or batches are produced within an accounting period. In this system, direct materials costs and direct labor costs can be directly related to jobs. Overhead is applied to jobs using a predetermined rate.

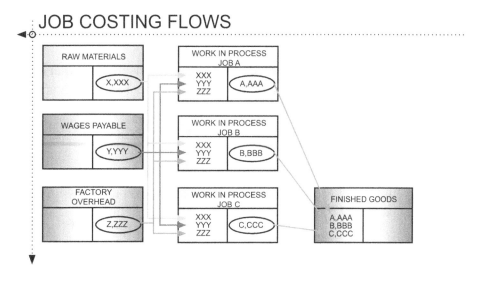

JOB COSTING FLOWS

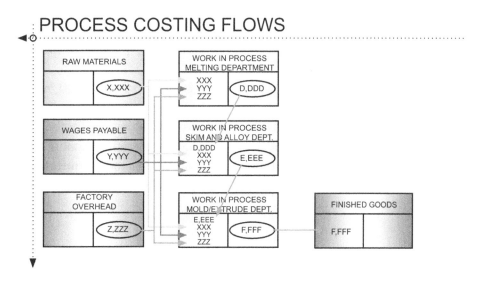

PROCESS COSTING FLOWS

Actual overhead costs are not traced to jobs. Examples of industries in which job-order costing is used include special order printing, shipbuilding, construction, hospitals, professional services such as law firms, and movie studios.

The chart above shows the cost flow for the process costing and job-order costing systems. As can be seen, the costs in the process costing system are attributed to processes whereas for a job-order costing system they are attributed to individual jobs.

Standard Costs and Variances

Some manufacturers choose to estimate the costs and assign it to the product rather than assigning the actual costs of direct material, direct labor, and manufacturing overhead. Such expected costs are called as *Standard Costs*. Thus, for such a manufacturer, the inventories and cost of goods sold begin with amounts reflecting the standard costs, not the actual costs, of a product. This can result in the estimated costs being different from the actual costs creating a *variance*.

Standard costing and the related variances is a useful tool that can be used by the management to assess how the planned costs compare with the actual costs. If a variance arises, management becomes aware that manufacturing costs have differed from the standard (planned, expected) costs.

- If actual costs are greater than standard costs the variance is unfavorable. An unfavorable variance tells management that if everything else stays constant the company's actual profit will be less than planned.

- If actual costs are less than standard costs the variance is favorable. A favorable variance tells management that if everything else stays constant the actual profit will likely exceed the planned profit.

The sooner that the accounting system reports a variance, the sooner that management can direct its attention to the difference from the planned amounts.

Example: Suppose February 2, 2006 ABC Inc. ordered 1000 bushels at $2.90 each. On February 8, 2006 ABC Inc. receives 1,000 bushels and an invoice for the actual cost of $2,900. On February 8 ABC Inc. inventory is increased by the standard cost of $3,000 (1,000 bushels at the standard cost of $3 per bushel), Accounts Payable is credited for $2,900 (the actual amount owed to the supplier), and the difference of $100 is credited to Direct Materials Price Variance. In general journal format the entry looks like this:

Inventory 3000
    Accounts Payable...2900
    Price Variance 100

On the other hand, had the actual cost of the bushel been $3.2 per bushel, the journal entries would be:

Inventory 3000
Price Variance 200
    Accounts Payable...3200

Use of Differential (Relevant) Cost

Relevant costs are defined as costs which are appropriate to making specific management decisions and are used by senior management in making operations, investment and strategic decisions.

Differential costs are defined as the cost differences between alternative courses of action and are also used by managements in making operations, investment and strategic decisions.

Example:

The following table shows the total cost of manufacturing widgets. The company is currently manufacturing 5 widgets per day and has received an offer to sell another widget for $50. Should the company accept the offer?

No. of Widgets	Total Cost
1	$ 60.00
2	$ 118.00
3	$ 165.00
4	$ 208.00
5	$ 250.00
6	$ 288.00
7	$ 315.00
8	$ 320.00

Solution:

In order to determine whether the firm should accept the offer, we need to focus on the relevant or differential costs which in this example would be the marginal costs.

No. of Widgets	Total Cost	Average Cost	Marginal Cost
1	$ 60.00	$ 60.00	$ 60.00
2	$ 118.00	$ 59.00	$ 58.00
3	$ 165.00	$ 55.00	$ 47.00
4	$ 208.00	$ 52.00	$ 43.00
5	$ 250.00	$ 50.00	$ 42.00
6	$ 288.00	$ 48.00	$ 38.00
7	$ 315.00	$ 45.00	$ 27.00
8	$ 320.00	$ 40.00	$ 5.00

As can be seen, the marginal cost of producing a sixth widget is $38 which is less than the price being offered and thus the company should accept the offer. Note that the average cost of $48 is more than the price being offered but this is not a relevant cost to make this decision and hence should not be considered.

BUSINESS ETHICS AND HOW IT APPLIES TO ACCOUNTING

Accountants can perform their work in many different areas, including auditing, managerial accounting, tax accounting, financial planning, consulting and, of course, simply preparing accounts. In each of these spheres, ethical issues appear and accountants perceive that opportunities exist in their work to engage in unethical behavior. Codes of conduct for accountants give guidelines for proper behavior in the profession. For accountants, as in any other profession, codes are the most concrete cultural form in which professions acknowledge their societal obligations. Codes of conduct contain a set of principles and rules, which specify what society expects to be considered in decision making. Codes of conduct are useful in several ways:

(1) Motivating through the use of peer pressure

(2) Providing a stable and permanent guide to right or wrong rather than leaving the question to continual ad hoc decisions

(3) Giving guidance, especially in ambiguous situations, guiding the behavior of the employees and controlling the autocratic power of employers over employees

(4) Helping to specify the social responsibility of business itself

(5) Contributing to the interest of business itself, for if businesses do not police themselves ethically, others will do it for them

The Code of Professional Conduct of the American Institute of Certified Public Accountants consists of two sections: (1) the Principles and (2) the Rules. The Principles provide the framework for the Rules, which govern the performance of professional services by members. The Council of the American Institute of Certified Public Accountants is authorized to designate bodies to promulgate technical standards under the Rules, and the bylaws require adherence to those Rules and standards.

The Code of Professional Conduct was adopted by the membership to provide guidance and rules to all members—those in public practice, in industry, in government, and in education—in the performance of their professional responsibilities.

Compliance with the Code of Professional Conduct, as with all standards in an open society, depends primarily on members' understanding and voluntary actions, secondarily on reinforcement by peers and public opinion, and ultimately on disciplinary proceedings, when necessary, against members who fail to comply with the Rules.

Accounting codes of conduct emphasize specific standards rather than generic principles. Some of the important rules proposed by the Code of Professional Conduct of the American Institute of Certified Public Accountants are:

Section 50 discusses the accounting profession's recognition of its responsibilities to the public, to clients, and to colleagues. They guide members in the performance of their professional responsibilities and express the basic tenets of ethical and professional conduct. The Principles call for a strict commitment to honorable behavior, even at the sacrifice of personal advantage.

Rule 101: This specifies that independence requires fulfilling the standards promulgated by bodies designated by the Council.

Rule 102: This specifies that objectivity and integrity involve being free of conflict of interests, and not knowingly misrepresenting facts and not subordinating one's judgments to others.

Section 200 talks about compliance in the general standards and accounting principles.

Section 300 discusses the responsibility to clients, including issues related with confidential client information and contingency fees.

Section 400 talks about responsibility to colleagues.

Section 500 talks about other responsibilities and practices.

FORMS OF BUSINESS

CORPORATION

A corporation is a legal entity which, while being composed of natural persons, exists completely separately from them. The scope of its status and capacity is determined by the law of the place of incorporation.

The most salient features of incorporation include:

LIMITED LIABILITY

Unlike in a partnership or sole proprietorship, members of a corporation hold no liability for the corporation's debts and obligations and their limited potential losses cannot exceed the amount which they contributed to the corporation.

PERPETUAL LIFETIME

The assets and structure of the corporation exist beyond the lifetime of any of its members or agents. This allows for stability and accumulation of capital, which thus becomes available for investment in projects of a larger size and over a longer term.

OWNERSHIP AND CONTROL

Humans and other legal entities can be members of corporations. In the case of for-profit corporations, these members hold shares and are thus called shareholders. When no members or shareholders exist, a corporation may exist as a "memberless corporation" or similar — this second type of corporation counts as a not-for-profit corporation. Typically, a board of directors governs a corporation on the behalf of the members. The corporate members elect the directors, and the board has a fiduciary duty to look after the interests of the corporation. The corporate officers such as the CEO, president, treasurer, and other titled officers are usually chosen by the board to manage the affairs of the corporation.

LIMITED LIABILITY COMPANY

A limited liability company (LLC) is a legal form of company offering limited liability to its owners. It is similar to a corporation, but is suitable for smaller companies with restricted numbers of owners.

Advantages of an LLC

- No requirement of an annual general meeting for shareholders.
- Less administrative paperwork and recordkeeping.
- No double taxation.
- Members are protected from liability for acts and debts of the LLC.
- Profits are taxed personally at the member level, not at the LLC level.

Disadvantages of an LLC

- Many states, including Alabama, California, Kentucky, New Jersey, New York, Pennsylvania, Tennessee, and Texas, levy a franchise tax or capital values tax on LLCs. The franchise tax can be an amount based on revenue, an amount based on profits, or an amount based on the number of owners or the amount of capital employed in the state, or some combination of those factors.
- It may be more difficult to raise capital for an LLC, as investors may be more comfortable investing funds in corporate form with an exit strategy of an eventual IPO.
- Average life span of an LLC is 30 years because of death of one of the owners. In some cases this rule can be bypassed if there is a consensus among all the other members and it is spelled out in an operating agreement.

LIMITED LIABILITY PARTNERSHIP

Limited liability partnerships (LLP) are a form of business organization combining elements of partnerships and corporations. In an LLP, all partners have a form of limited liability, similar to that of the shareholders of a corporation. However, the partners have the right to manage the business directly.

Limited liability partnerships are distinct from limited partnerships, in that limited liability is granted to all partners, not to a subset of non-managing "limited partners." As a result the LLP is more suited for businesses where all investors wish to take an active role in management. Although found in many business fields, the LLP is an especially popular form of organization among professionals, particularly lawyers, accountants and architects.

🎓 *Sample Test Questions*

1) Which of the following is not an assumption made by GAAP?

    A) Economic Entity Assumption
    B) Going Concern Assumption
    C) Double Entry Assumption
    D) Monetary Unit Assumption
    E) Periodic Reporting Assumption

The correct answer is C:) Double Entry Assumption.

2) According to FASB, _____ is the process of reporting a transaction in the financial statements.

    A) Recognition
    B) Journal Entry
    C) Adjusting Entry
    D) Realization
    E) Allocation

The correct answer is B:) Journal Entry.

3) The accounting cycle has the following key steps:

    (i)   Journal Entry
    (ii) Adjusting Entry
    (iii) Trial Balance
    (iv) Closing Entry
    (v) Adjusted Trial Balance

Which of the following represents the correct sequence of steps?

    A) i,iii,ii,v,iv
    B) i,iv,iii,ii,v
    C) i,ii,iii,v,iv
    D) i,iii,ii,iv,v
    E) iii,i,ii,v,iv

The correct answer is A:) i,iii,ii,v,iv.

4) Margie Gift Certificates Inc. sold gift certificates with an expiry period of one year and worth $500,000 in the year 2005. It is estimated that 8% of the gift certificates will not be redeemed. Of the gift certificates sold, $300,000 was redeemed in the year 2006. What will be the unearned revenue reported by the company in its balance sheet for the year 2006?

    A) $200,000
    B) $300,000
    C) $40,000
    D) $160,000
    E) $460,000

The correct answer is D:) $160,000.

5) Which of the following occur at acquisition cost in the balance sheet?

    A) Monetary assets
    B) Non-monetary assets
    C) Retained earnings
    D) All of the above
    E) None of the above

The correct answer is B:) Non-monetary assets.

6) In statement of cash flows, interest payments are classified as cash outflows under _____ section.

    A) Operating activities
    B) Borrowing activities
    C) Lending activities
    D) Financing activities
    E) Investing activities

The correct answer is A:) Operating activities.

7) Which of the following is TRUE?

    A) A bond priced at less than par has the yield to maturity more than the coupon rate of the bond

    B) A bond priced at more than par has the yield to maturity more than the coupon rate of the bond

    C) A bond priced at less than par has the yield to maturity less than the coupon rate of the bond

    D) All of the above

    E) None of the above

The correct answer is A:) A bond priced at less than par has the yield to maturity more than the coupon rate of the bond.

8) The price of a bond depends upon

    A) Coupon rate

    B) Discount rate

    C) Par Value

    D) A, B & C

    E) A & C

The correct answer is D:) A, B & C.

9) Company XYZ sells a bicycle for cash and records it with a journal entry which includes the following adjustments: Sales Revenue for $300, Inventory for $150 and Cash for $300. Cost of goods sold must have been

    A) $600

    B) $450

    C) $300

    D) $150

    E) Cannot be determined

The correct answer is D:) $150. The journal entry would be a debit to Cash and credit to sales revenue each for $300, and a debit to COGS and credit inventory each for $150.

10) The Sarbanes-Oxley Act requires companies to

A) Publish a statement of cash flows
B) Give their employees pay raises each year
C) Maintain adequate environmental practices
D) Reduce pollution by 4%
E) Implement internal controls

The correct answer is E:) Implement internal controls. For example, hiring an auditor to review financial statements is an example of internal controls.

11) Credits are recorded on

A) The right side of a T account
B) The bottom of the income statement
C) The bottom of the balance sheet
D) The left side of a T account
E) None of the above

The correct answer is A:) The right side of a T account. Debits would be recorded on the right side.

12) On August 21, Company ABC purchased 500 dollars of inventory on account from their suppliers. Which of the following would be included in the journal entry to record the purchase?

A) Credit to inventory
B) Debit to accounts receivable
C) Credit to accounts payable
D) Debit to cash
E) Both A and B

The correct answer is C:) Credit to accounts payable. Buying on account incurs a liability (accounts payable) which is increased with a credit and offset by a debit to inventory.

13) Which of the following is represented by the goodwill account on the balance sheet?

    A) A company's homegrown goodwill
    B) The goodwill of other companies that were bought out
    C) The goodwill of the owner's
    D) Both A and B
    E) Both A and C

The correct answer is B:) The goodwill of other companies that were bought out. Goodwill is determined as anything above the physical value of the company (it's assets less liabilities) that was paid to obtain it. A company's home grown goodwill is not reflected on financial statements.

14) Which principle states that an accounting rule may be violated if the amount is irrelevant?

    A) Conservatism
    B) Cost
    C) Full disclosure
    D) Materiality
    E) Objectivity

The correct answer is D:) Materiality. This is the reason that financial statements typically have rounded values.

15) Which principle states that if there are two acceptable ways of recording something, the one which will result in the lowest net income should be chosen?

    A) Conservatism
    B) Cost
    C) Full disclosure
    D) Materiality
    E) Objectivity

The correct answer is A:) Conservatism. This principle also extends to the option that will result in the lowest asset total.

16) Which principle states that values should be recorded at their historical cost?

    A) Conservatism
    B) Cost
    C) Full disclosure
    D) Materiality
    E) Objectivity

The correct answer is B:) Cost.

17) Which principle states that any additional important information should be disclosed on the financial statements?

    A) Conservatism
    B) Cost
    C) Full disclosure
    D) Materiality
    E) Objectivity

The correct answer is C:) Full disclosure. This is the reason that financial statements will often have asterisks with additional information about a reported value.

18) Which of the following is true for accrual basis of accounting?

    A) The accrual basis of accounting recognizes the revenue when the firm sells goods or renders services.
    B) In the accrual basis of accounting, a firm recognizes revenues from selling goods and services in the period when it receives cash from customers.
    C) The costs of assets used in producing revenues lead to expenses in the period when the firm recognizes the revenues that the costs helped produce.
    D) A, B & C
    E) A & C

The correct answer is E:) A & C.

19) Which of the following is true for expense recognition?

   A) If asset expiration associates directly with particular revenue, that expiration becomes an expense in the period when the firm recognizes the revenue.
   B) If asset expiration does not clearly associate with revenues, that expiration becomes an expense of the period when the firm consumes the benefits of the asset in operation.
   C) If asset expiration does not clearly associate with revenues, that expiration becomes an expense at the end of the accounting period.
   D) A & B
   E) A & C

The correct answer is D:) A & B.

20) Which of the following is true for a year in which the purchases exceeded the overall sales of the firm?

   A) The quantity of units in inventory decreases
   B) A firm using FIFO will be concerned about potential reduction in taxes
   C) A firm using LIFO will be concerned about potential reduction in taxes
   D) A & B
   E) A & C

The correct answer is C:) A firm using LIFO will be concerned about potential reduction in taxes.

21) If the Board of Directors for a company decides to issue dividends, which of the following will occur?

   A) Assets will increase
   B) Liabilities will decrease
   C) Liabilities will increase
   D) Retained earnings will decrease
   E) Retained earnings will increase

The correct answer is D:) Retained earnings will decrease. Retained earnings is equal to net income less dividends. If dividends increase then retained earnings will decrease.

22) If a company issues bonds

    A) Liabilities will increase
    B) Liabilities will decrease
    C) Owner's equity will increase
    D) Owner's equity will decrease
    E) Assets will decrease

The correct answer is A:) Liabilities will increase. Bonds are a type of loan and therefore affect liabilities.

23) Which of the formulas represents net sales?

    A) Sales Revenues – Sales Returns and Allowances
    B) Revenue – Cost of Goods Sold
    C) Beginning Inventory + Inventory Purchased – Cost of Goods Sold
    D) Beginning Inventory + Cost of Goods Purchased + Cost of Goods Manufactured
    E) None of the above

The correct answer is A:) Sales Revenues – Sales Returns and Allowances. This represents the total value of goods the company sold.

24) Which of the formulas represents gross profit?

    A) Sales Revenues – Sales Returns and Allowances
    B) Revenue – Cost of Goods Sold
    C) Beginning Inventory + Inventory Purchased – Cost of Goods Sold
    D) Beginning Inventory + Cost of Goods Purchased + Cost of Goods Manufactured
    E) None of the above

The correct answer is B:) Revenue – Cost of Goods Sold. This represents the actual gains that the company made in selling its inventory.

25) A write-off is recorded with a

    A) Debit to accounts receivable
    B) Credit to bad debt expense
    C) Debit to allowance for bad debts
    D) Credit to allowance for bad debts
    E) None of the above

The correct answer is C:) Debit to allowance for bad debts. Instead of counting the write-off as an expense, the amount is removed from allowance for bad debts with a debit and accounts receivable with a credit.

26) With the percentage of sales method of accounting for bad debts, bad debts are recorded with a

    A) Debit to Bad Debt Expense and Credit to Allowance for Bad Debt
    B) Credit to Bad Debt Expense and Debit to Allowance for Bad Debt
    C) Debit to Bad Debt Expense and Credit to Accounts Receivable
    D) Credit to bad Debt Expense and Debit to Accounts Receivable
    E) None of the above

The correct answer is A:) Debit to Bad Debt Expense and Credit to Allowance for Bad Debt.

27) Which of the following is a contra asset account?

    A) Sales returns and allowances
    B) Cash
    C) Notes payable
    D) Accumulated Depreciation
    E) None of the above

The correct answer is D:) Accumulated Depreciation. Accumulated depreciation is listed as an asset, but has the effect of reducing the value of assets making it a contra asset account.

28) A financial statement prepared in conformity with generally accepted accounting is used by investors and creditors whereas a managerial accounting report is more likely to:

    A) Be used by decision makers external to the organization.
    B) Details the operation results of the last accounting period.
    C) View the entire organization as the reporting entity.
    D) Be tailored to the specific needs of an individual decision maker.
    E) Assist in generating cash flow projections for the next year.

The correct answer is D:) Be tailored to the specific needs of an individual decision maker.

29) Which of the following is true about income statements and balance sheet?

    A) Income statements provide information for a period of time whereas balance sheet provides information at a point in time
    B) Income statements provide information at a point in time whereas balance sheet provides information for a period of time
    C) Income statement and balance sheet are related to each other through the statement of cash flows
    D) Income statements provide information for the end of the year whereas balance sheet provides information at a point in time
    E) Income statements provide information for the beginning of the year whereas balance sheet provides information at a point in time

The correct answer is A:) Income statements provide information for a period of time whereas balance sheet provides information at a point in time.

30) The matching principle is best characterized as:

    A) Assets = Liabilities + Shareholder's equity
    B) Is used to determine the proper period for recognition of expenses
    C) Is used to determine the proper period for recognition of revenue
    D) Is used to offset the cash receipts of the period with the cash payments made during the period
    E) None of the above

The correct answer is B:) Is used to determine the proper period for recognition of expenses.

31) Which of the following is true for dividends and expenses?

    A) All dividend and expense transactions involve offsetting credit entries to the Cash account.
    B) Both expenses and dividends are offset against revenue in the income statement.
    C) Both expenses and dividends reduce owner's equity.
    D) Expenses reduce owner's equity while dividends do not have any impact to the owner's equity.
    E) Neither expenses nor dividends reduce owner's equity.

The correct answer is C:) Both expenses and dividends reduce owner's equity.

32) ABC Inc. finds that goods purchased on account are defective and returns them to the supplier. The entry to record this return will reduce ABC Inc.:

    A) Sales revenue and the cost of goods sold.
    B) Inventory and Account Payable.
    C) Inventory and cost of goods sold.
    D) Sales revenue and Account Receivable.
    E) Inventory and Account Receivable.

The correct answer is B:) Inventory and Account Payable.

33) Why are intangible assets amortized?

    A) Because they increase in value over time.
    B) Because their value is only recognized as they are used.
    C) Because they have a limited useful life.
    D) They aren't, the full value is eliminated at once.
    E) None of the above

The correct answer is C:) Because they have a limited useful life. Patents, copyrights and trademarks all expire after a set number of years, therefore amortization is recorded each year until that point.

34) A patent with a useful life of 10 years is purchased for $20,000. At the end of the third year, what is the balance in the accumulated amortization account, assuming the straight line method of accounting is used?

A) $2,000 credit balance
B) $6,000 credit balance
C) $2,000 debit balance
D) $6,000 debit balance
E) $20,000 debit balance

The correct answer is B:) $6,000 credit balance. The patent would amortize at a rate of $20,000/10 or $2,000 per year. After three years, that would be six thousand dollars.

35) Based on the following information what is the quick ratio for Company A?

Cash   150
Accounts Receivable   190
Accounts Payable   65
Short Term Loan Payable   30
Inventory   500
Interest Payable   15
Long Term Debt   160
Land, Buildings, Machinery   350
Capital Stock   100

A) 1.36
B) 2.05
C) 3.09
D) 6.15
E) 7.63

The correct answer is C:) 3.09. (Cash+Accounts Receivable)/(Accounts Payable + Short Term Loan Payable + Interest Payable)= 3.09.

36) A company decides to pay their insurance three months in advance and the payment is recorded as prepaid insurance. Which of the following increased as a result?

   A) Insurance Expense
   B) Assets
   C) Liabilities
   D) Owner's Equity
   E) Both A and C

The correct answer is B:) Assets. Prepaid insurance is an asset, therefore increasing it would increase assets.

37) If prepaid expense is decreased as expenses are incurred, then

   A) Expenses increase
   B) Liabilities decrease
   C) Owner's equity increases
   D) Assets decrease
   E) Both A and D

The correct answer is E:) Both A and D. Prepaid expense is an asset so decreasing it decreases assets. Expenses are increased as the balance is transferred from prepaid expense when the expenses occur.

38) Trading securities are recorded on the balance sheet at their

   A) Historical cost
   B) Fair value
   C) Market cost
   D) Net realizable value
   E) None of the above

The correct answer is C:) Market cost. This is done be revaluating the value of the securities each time the balance sheet is redone.

39) Using the following information, determine the accounts receivable turnover for Year 2:

	Year 1	Year 2
Sales Revenue	$15,000	$21,000
Net Credit Sales	$10,000	$15,000
Net Cash Sales	$5,000	$6,000
Accounts receivable	$7,000	$8,500

A) 1.76
B) 1.93
C) 2.71
D) 3.21
E) None of the above

The correct answer is B:) 1.93. Net Credit Sales for Year 2 = $15,000. Average accounts receivable = $7,750. $15000/$7750 = 1.93.

40) Use the following information to determine the accounts receivable turnover for Year 2:

	Year 1	Year 2
Sales Revenue	$15,000	$8,000
Net Cash Sales	$11,000	$2,000
Accounts receivable	$3,000	$2,500

A) 3.2
B) .72
C) 2.4
D) 2.18
E) None of the above

The correct answer is D:) 2.18. Average accounts receivable = $2,750. Net Credit Sales for Year 2 = $6,000. $6000/$2750=2.81.

41) Which of the following accounts would need to be closed out at the end of the year?

    A) Cash
    B) Short term loans payable
    C) Sales revenue
    D) Accounts receivable
    E) None of the above

The correct answer is C:) Sales revenue. Sales revenue is a nominal account and should be closed out at the end of the year.

42) The year that a company uses when preparing financial statements is called the

    A) Fiscal year
    B) Financial year
    C) Budget year
    D) All of the above
    E) None of the above

The correct answer is D:) All of the above. Fiscal year, financial year and budget year are all terms referred to the year period which companies and governments chose to prepare their financial statements around.

43) Which GAAP assumption refers to the company continuing to operate in the future?

    A) Accounting entity
    B) Going concern
    C) Objectivity
    D) Time period principle
    E) Monetary unit principle

The correct answer is B:) Going concern. This is the assumption that the company will operate indefinitely.

44) Which of the following is NOT one of the four basic GAAP assumptions?

A) Accounting entity
B) Going concern
C) Objectivity
D) Time period principle
E) Monetary unit principle

The correct answer is C:) Objectivity. The four basic GAAP assumptions are accounting entity, going concern, time-period principle and the monetary unit principle.

45) Retained earnings will decrease if

A) Revenues increase
B) Expenses decrease
C) Net income increases
D) Dividends decrease
E) Expenses increase

The correct answer is E:) Expenses increase. Increasing expenses would decrease net income which would decrease retained earnings.

46) Which of the following is a contra revenue account?

A) Sales returns and allowances
B) Cash
C) Notes payable
D) Depreciation
E) None of the above

The correct answer is A:) Sales returns and allowance. The purpose of this account is to reduce sales revenues, making it a contra account, and specifically a contra revenue account.

47) Which of the following statements is FALSE?

A) Revenues regularly has a credit balance
B) Expenses regularly has a credit balance
C) Loans payable regularly has a credit balance
D) Accounts receivable regularly has a debit balance
E) Inventory regularly has a debit balance

The correct answer is B:) Expenses regularly has a credit balance. Expenses reduce equity and therefore are recorded with a debit, not a credit.

48) Company A is just starting up and takes out a $200,000 business loan to finance their company. In addition, the owner of Company A contributes $100,000 of his own savings. Assuming that nothing else changes, what is the balance in the asset account when a $15,000 dollar expenses is incurred?

    A) $315,000
    B) $300,000
    C) $285,000
    D) $215,000
    E) ($15,000)

The correct answer is C:) $285,000. Assets = Liabilities + Owners Equity. Company A incurred $200,000 liability and contributed $100,000 owner's equity, but owner's equity was reduced by $15,000 resulting in a total of $285,000.

49) If assets increase by $35,000 and liabilities decrease by $10,000, what change must have occurred in the owner's equity account?

    A) Increase $25,000
    B) Decrease $25,000
    C) Increase $45,000
    D) Decrease $45,000
    E) None of the above

The correct answer is C:) Increase $45,000. This can be found using the basic accounting equation: Assets = Liabilities –Owner's Equity.

50) Which of the following accounts would decrease with a debit?

    A) Cost of goods sold
    B) Cash
    C) Prepaid insurance
    D) Inventory
    E) Loan payable

The correct answer is E:) Loan payable. A loan payable account would be representative of a liability and would therefore be increased with a credit and decreased with a debit.

51) ABC Inc. and XYZ Inc. purchased identical plant assets with a useful life of 10 years and no salvage value. ABC Inc. uses straight-line depreciation in its financial statements, whereas XYZ Inc. uses an accelerated method. Which of the following statements is correct?

   A) Over the life of the asset, XYZ Inc. will recognize more depreciation expense than ABC Inc.
   B) In the tenth year, ABC Inc. will recognize more depreciation expense on this asset than XYZ Inc.
   C) If the asset is sold after 4 years, ABC Inc. is more likely to report a gain than is XYZ Inc.
   D) In its income tax return, only XYZ Inc. may depreciate this asset by the MACRS method.
   E) In the fifth year, both XYZ Inc. and ABC Inc. will report the same depreciation in their financial statements.

The correct answer is B:) In the tenth year, ABC Inc. will recognize more depreciation expense on this asset than XYZ Inc.

52) Which of the following transactions would have no impact on stockholders' equity?

   A) Purchase of a building from the proceeds of a bank loan.
   B) Dividends to shareholders
   C) Net loss
   D) Investments of cash by stockholders
   E) Repurchase of stocks

The correct answer is A:) Purchase of a building from the proceeds of a bank loan.

53) ABC Inc. had beginning shareholders' equity of $160,000. During the year business operations resulted in an increase of assets by $240,000 and an increase of liabilities by $120,000. The net income for the year was computed as $180,000. If no additional investments were made, the dividends issued were

   A) $20,000
   B) $60,000
   C) $140,000
   D) $220,000
   E) $280,000

The correct answer is B:) $60,000.

54) Which of the following is not a right accorded to the shareholders?

 A) Preemptive right
 B) Voting rights
 C) Preference in liquidation
 D) Transferability of shares
 E) All of the above

The correct answer is C:) Preference in liquidation.

55) ABC Inc. has 500,000 shares of common stock outstanding. On May 15, the board of directors declared a $0.80 per share cash dividend, to be paid to stockholders on October 12. The dividend was distributed on November 11. The proper journal entry to record on November 11 is:

 A) Dividends Expense 400,000
    Cash 400,000
 B) Dividends Payable 400,000
    Cash 400,000
 C) Retained Earnings 400,000
    Cash 400,000
 D) Dividends Payable 400,000
    Retained Earnings 400,000
 E) Cash 500,000
    Dividends Expense 500,000

The correct answer is B:) Dividends Payable 400,000, Cash 400,000.

56) XYZ Inc. has 500,000 shares of common stock authorized. The stock has a par value of $1.50 per share, and 150,000 shares are outstanding. XYZ Inc. declares a 5% stock dividend on May 6. The market value of the stock on May 6 is $7 per share. How should this be recorded as a Journal entry?

A) No entry

B) Retained Earnings   11,250
   Common Stock   11,250

C) Retained Earnings   52,500
   Stock Dividend Distributable   11,250
   Paid-in Capital in Excess of Par   41,250

D) Stock Dividends Payable   11,250
   Retained Earnings   41,250
   Common Stock   52,500

E) Retained Earnings   52,500
   Common Stock   52,500

The correct answer is C:) Retained Earnings 52,500, Stock Dividend Distributable 11,250, Paid-in Capital in Excess of Par 41,250.

57) Which of the following accounts would regularly have a credit balance?

A) Unearned revenue
B) Prepaid rent
C) Cost of goods sold
D) Accounts receivable
E) Interest expense

The correct answer is A:) Unearned revenue. Unearned revenue is recorded as a liability and would therefore have a credit balance.

58) Which of the following accounts would regularly have a debit balance?

A) Revenue
B) Loan payable
C) Unearned revenue
D) Accounts receivable
E) None of the above

The correct answer is D:) Accounts receivable.

59) When doing bank reconciliation a company notices that the bank processed a check for 215 dollars for 251 dollars instead. They should

A) Change their records to match those of the bank to avoid paperwork.
B) Ignore the problem and hope that the records match up again later on.
C) Inform the bank of the mistake and have them make the necessary adjustments.
D) Both B and C
E) None of the above

The correct answer is C:) Inform the bank of the mistake and have them make the necessary adjustments. The company's financial statements should not change because they are correct.

60) During bank reconciliation what should be done regarding outstanding checks?

A) Nothing. The records will correct themselves with time.
B) The company's records should be changed to match the banks until the check clears.
C) The checks should be subtracted from the bank's statements.
D) Outstanding checks are irrelevant because they are always recorded simultaneously by the company and the bank.
E) None of the above

The correct answer is C:) The checks should be subtracted from the bank's statements.

61) Which of the following would be used by a company to keep track of the accounts used in their general ledger?

A) Chart of accounts
B) Memory
C) T account
D) Account tracker chart
E) None of the above

The correct answer is A:) Chart of accounts. The chart of accounts is a document which lists the accounts referenced in the general ledger and assigns them a unique number to be identified by.

62) On July 1, 2001, XYZ Inc. purchased a new machine for $200,000 with an estimated useful life of 10 years and a salvage value of $5,000. XYZ Inc. uses straight-line depreciation. However, during 2005, the company realized that the machine would not be efficient to operate after December 31, 2007. In addition, the machine would have no scrap value. How much should be charged to depreciation expense in 2005 under generally accepted accounting principles?

   A) $19,500
   B) $5,000
   C) $43,917
   D) $65,000
   E) $12,174

The correct answer is C:) $43,917.

63) Which of the following describes quick assets?

   A) Assets - Liabilities
   B) Assets - Current Assets
   C) Assets - Inventory
   D) Current Assets - Inventory
   E) Current Assets - Current Liabilities

The correct answer is D:) Current Assets - Inventory. The value of current assets less inventories is referred to as quick assets because of its use in the quick ratio.

64) Which board creates the basic rules of accounting?

   A) GAAP
   B) FASB
   C) International Standards of Accounting Board
   D) General Accounting Bylaw Commissions Board
   E) None of the above

The correct answer is B:) FASB. FASB stands for Financial Accounting Standards Board.

65) Which of the following is the standard which United States companies must adhere to in their accounting practices?

    A) GAAP
    B) FASB
    C) National Accounting Standard
    D) General Accounting Commission Principles
    E) None of the above

The correct answer is A:) GAAP. GAAP stands for Generally Accepted Accounting Principles and is put together by the FASB.

66) Which of the following is false?

    A) Goodwill is the difference between the price paid to purchase a particular company, and the fair value of the underlying identifiable assets received.
    B) Goodwill should not be amortized, but be evaluated for impairment.
    C) Goodwill is an intangible asset.
    D) Goodwill may be recorded for a company whether it is internally generated or purchased.
    E) Goodwill should be recorded only when it is purchased.

The correct answer is D:) Goodwill may be recorded for a company whether it is internally generated or purchased.

67) Which of the following are drawbacks associated with the direct write-off method of recording uncollectible accounts?

    A) It does not usually recognize the loss in the period in which the sale occurs and the firm recognizes the revenue.
    B) It provides the firm with an opportunity to manipulate earnings each period by deciding when particular customers' accounts become uncollectible.
    C) The amount of accounts receivable on the balance sheet does not reflect the amount a firm expects to collect in cash.
    D) A, C
    E) A, B, C

The correct answer is E:) A, B, C.

68) Which of the following is true regarding depreciation?

    A) The term depreciation refers to the charge made to the current operations for the portion of the cost of such assets consumed during the current period.
    B) Accumulated depreciation is an income statement account.
    C) Accumulated depreciation includes the cumulative depreciation charges since the firm acquired the assets.
    D) A, C
    E) A, B, C

The correct answer is D:) A, C.

69) A firm uses the percentage-of-completion method to recognize income. This firm is building a hotel in Los Angeles downtown for $100 million. It is estimated that the firm would make a 20% profit. The expenses would be distributed as below:

Year 1: 25% of total expense
Year 2: 20% of total expense
Year 3: 30% of total expense
Year 4: 25% of total expense

What would the income and expense be recorded in year 3:

    A) 30 million, 24 million
    B) 30 million, 30 million
    C) 30 million, 20 million
    D) 20 million, 24 million
    E) 20 million, 30 million

The correct answer is A:) 30 million, 24 million.

70) Which of the following disclosures are required by FASB Statement No. 115?

    A) The aggregate market value, gross unrealized holding gains, gross unrealized holding losses and amortized cost for debt securities held to maturity and debt and equity securities available for sale.
    B) The proceeds from sales of securities available for sale and the gross realized gains and the gross realized losses on those sales.
    C) The change during the period in the net unrealized holding gain or loss on securities available for sale included in a separate shareholder's equity account.
    D) The change during the period in the net unrealized holding gain or loss on trading securities included in earnings.
    E) All of the above

The correct answer is E:) All of the above.

71) Jack, Jill and Henry are partners in a professional services firm. Jack' contribution in the partnership is $60,000; Jill's is $15,000; Henry's is $75,000. The partnership uses the ratio of capital investments method to split the earnings. What will be the share of Jack, Jill and Henry?

    A) 40%, 15%, 55%
    B) 40%, 10%, 50%
    C) $60,000; $15,000; $75,000
    D) 35%, 25%, 40%
    E) 60%, 10%, 30%

The correct answer is B:) 40%, 10%, 50%.

72) Which of the following is true for full cost accounting?

    A) Accounting for costs rather than outlays
    B) Accounting for hidden costs and externalities
    C) Accounting for overhead and indirect costs
    D) Accounting for past and future outlays
    E) All of the above

The correct answer is E:) All of the above.

73) Contribution Margin is defined as

   A) Contribution Margin is equal to sales revenues less variable costs
   B) Contribution Margin is equal to sales revenues less total costs
   C) Contribution Margin is equal to sales revenues less fixed costs
   D) Contribution Margin is the same as net profit
   E) Contribution Margin is the net profit before tax

The correct answer is A:) Contribution Margin is equal to sales revenues less variable costs.

74) XYZ Inc. manufactures widgets. Each unit retails at $2.5. It costs XYZ Inc. $1 to make each one, and the fixed costs for the period are $600. What is the break-even point in units and in sales revenue?

   A) 400, $400
   B) 400, $1,000
   C) 240, $600
   D) 600, $1,500
   E) 100, $2,500

The correct answer is B:) 400, $1,000.

75) ABC Inc. had accounts receivable of $33,000 at the end of the last year. In the current year, total sales were $505,000 and the cash collected was $520,000. What is the account receivable at the end of the current year?

   A) $33,000
   B) $48,000
   C) $18,000
   D) -$15,000
   E) $15,000

The correct answer is C:) $18,000.

76) Which of the following is true for Economic Value Added (EVA)?

    A) EVA = After-tax operating income – (estimated cost of capital × Total capital employed)

    B) EVA = After-tax operating income – (estimated percentage cost of capital × Total capital employed)

    C) EVA = After-tax operating income – (actual percentage cost of capital × Total capital employed)

    D) EVA = Before-tax operating income – (actual percentage cost of capital × Total capital employed)

    E) EVA = Before-tax operating income – (estimated percentage cost of capital × Total capital employed)

The correct answer is C:) EVA = After-tax operating income – (actual percentage cost of capital × Total capital employed).

77) Which of the following are the perspectives for measuring operational and financial performance per the balanced scorecard?

    A) Financial perspective - describes the economic consequences of actions taken in the other three perspectives.

    B) Customer perspective - defines the customer and market segments in which the business operates.

    C) Internal business process perspective - describes the internal processes needed to provide value for customers and owners.

    D) Learning and growth perspective - defines the capabilities that an organization needs to create long-term growth and improvement.

    E) All of the above

The correct answer is E:) All of the above.

78) Which of the following are true for process costing systems?

    A) This system is usually used in companies which produce a single, homogeneous product or service.

    B) This system is used when different types of products, jobs, or batches are produced within an accounting period.

    C) In this system, total manufacturing costs are divided by total number of units produced during a given period.

    D) A & C

    E) B & C

The correct answer is D:) A & C.

79) ABC Inc. had an operating income of $3.2 million in the year 2005. In the beginning of 2005, the net book value of the operating assets was $48 million and at the end of the year, the net book value was $32 million. What is the ROI of ABC Inc. in 2005?

    A) 10%
    B) 16.67%
    C) 8%
    D) 3.2%
    E) 9%

The correct answer is C:) 8%.

80) What are the differences in profit calculations using absorption costing and direct costing?

    A) If beginning and ending inventory are the same, absorption costing profit = direct costing profit
    B) If ending inventory is lower than beginning inventory, direct costing profit < absorption costing profit
    C) If ending inventory is higher than beginning inventory, direct costing profit > absorption costing profit
    D) A, B & C
    E) B & C

The correct answer is A:) If beginning and ending inventory are the same, absorption costing profit = direct costing profit.

81) Suppose on June 2, 2006 ABC Inc. ordered 1000 bushels at $1.90 each. On June 8, 2006 ABC Inc. receives 1,000 bushels and an invoice for the actual cost of $1,900. On June 8 ABC Inc. inventory is increased by the standard cost of $2,000 (1,000 bushels at the standard cost of $2 per bushel). The journal entry to record the above is:

A) Inventory 2000
    Price Variance 900
        Accounts Payable..2900
B) Inventory 2000
        Accounts Payable..1900
        Price Variance 100
C) Inventory 2000
    Price Variance 100
        Accounts Payable..2100
D) Inventory 1900
    Price Variance 100
        Accounts Payable..2000
E) Inventory 2000
        Accounts Receivable...1900
        Price Variance 100

The correct answer is B:)
    Inventory 2000
        Accounts Payable..1900
        Price Variance 100

82) Which of the following is true about standard variance?

A) If actual costs are greater than standard costs the variance is unfavorable.
B) A variance tells the management that manufacturing costs have differed from the standard (planned, expected) costs.
C) If actual costs are less than standard costs the variance is favorable.
D) A & B
E) A, B & C

The correct answer is A:) If actual costs are greater than standard costs the variance is unfavorable.

83) ABC Inc. incurred the following costs during 2005:

Accounting and legal fees	$100,000
Freight-in	$75,000
Freight-out	$45,000
Officers Salaries	$50,000
Insurance	$20,000
Sales representative salaries	$80,000

What amount of these costs should be reported as general and administrative expenses for the year 2005?

A) $170,000
B) $250,000
C) $370,000
D) $120,000
E) $180,000

The correct answer is A:) $170,000.

84) XYZ Inc. had 100 units of item Q on hand at Jan 1, 2005. Unit cost of each of these items was $15. Purchase of item Q during the year are as below:

Date	Units	Price
Mar 1	80	$20
May 1	40	$25
June 1	60	$30

On Jan 1, 2006 the inventory of item Q was 200. If XYZ Inc. uses LIFO, what is the cost of the inventory?

A) $3,700
B) $3,600
C) $4,200
D) $3,400
E) $3,900

The correct answer is B:) $3,600.

85) ABC Inc. purchased XYZ Inc. at a cost that resulted in recognition of good will of $120,000. ABC Inc. spent an additional $30,000 on expenditures to maintain goodwill. What amount should be reported as goodwill at the end of the year?

   A) $30,000
   B) $90,000
   C) $120,000
   D) $150,000
   E) None of the above

The correct answer is C:) $120,000.

86) ABC Inc. requires advance payments before it starts manufacturing the equipment. The advance information for the year 2005 is as below:

Customer advances as of Jan 1, 2005	$150,000
Advances received with orders in 2005	$250,000
Advances applied to orders shipped in 2005	$300,000
Advances applied to cancelled orders	$10,000

What is the current liability related to customer advances at the end of 2005?

   A) $90,000
   B) $100,000
   C) $110,000
   D) $150,000
   E) $190,000

The correct answer is A:) $90,000.

87) ABC Inc. had 1,000,000 shares of common stock outstanding on Jan 1, 2005. During 2005, ABC Inc. issued 200,000 additional shares of common stock. ABC Inc. reported net income of $2,500,000 in 2005 and paid $100,000 as preferred stock dividends. What is the earnings per share at the end of year 2005?

   A) 2.5
   B) 2.1
   C) 2.0
   D) 1.8
   E) None of the above

The correct answer is C:) 2.0.

88) XYZ Inc. suffered damage to its manufacturing plant. The building cost of the plant was $250,000 with an accumulated depreciation of $150,000. XYZ received claim from the insurance company and reported an extraordinary loss of $45,000. What will be the net change reported in the cash flows from investing activities section?

   A) $45,000
   B) $55,000
   C) $105,000
   D) $145,000
   E) $250,000

The correct answer is B:) $55,000.

89) How would stockholder's equity be affected by the declaration of

	Stock Dividend	Stock Split
A)	No effect	Increase
B)	Decrease	Increase
C)	Decrease	Decrease
D)	No effect	No effect
E)	Increase	Increase

The correct answer is D:) No effect, No effect.

90) If the following are the balance sheet changes:

$3,005 decrease in accounts receivable
$1,012 decrease in notes payable
$1,001 increase in accounts payable
$1,950 decrease in net fixed assets

a "use" of funds would be:

A) $3,005
B) $1,012
C) $1,001
D) $1,950
E) None of the above

The correct answer is B:) $1,012.

91) XYZ Inc. had a net increase of $80,000 in net fixed assets over the last period. The beginning and ending net fixed asset account balances were $100,000 and 180,000 respectively. If the firm purchased $200,000 in additional fixed assets and sold $100,000 of fixed assets at book value, what was the firm's depreciation expense over the period?

A) $20,000
B) $80,000
C) $100,000
D) $180,000
E) $200,000

The correct answer is A:) $20,000.

92) ABC Inc. paid $80,000 in dividends over the last period. The beginning and ending retained earnings account balances were $1,000,000 and $1,500,000 respectively. Assuming a 40% average tax rate, what was the firm's net income?

A) $500,000
B) $420,000
C) $580,000
D) $80,000
E) $480,000

The correct answer is C:) $580,000.

93) Which statement would be used to determine how efficiently a company uses cash resources?

    A) Statement of Retained Earnings
    B) Balance Sheet
    C) Income Statement
    D) Statement of Cash Flows
    E) None of the above

The correct answer is D:) Statement of Cash Flows. This statement catalogs all inflows and outflows of cash during a period, and categorizes them. Therefore, it can be used to determine how efficiently cash is being used.

94) Which statement would be used to determine which expenses were the greatest during a fiscal period?

    A) Statement of Retained Earnings
    B) Balance Sheet
    C) Income Statement
    D) Statement of Cash Flows
    E) None of the above

The correct answer is C:) Income Statement. Revenues and expenses are all cataloged on the income statement so that the net income or loss can be calculated.

95) Which statement would be used to determine how a company is funded?

    A) Statement of Retained Earnings
    B) Balance Sheet
    C) Income Statement
    D) Statement of Cash Flows
    E) None of the above

The correct answer is B:) Balance Sheet. The balance sheet will display the totals of equity and any loans that have been taken out by the company. This information can be used to determine how the company has leveraged itself.

96) In preparation for compiling completed financial statements, what is created to display the final balances in each ledger account?

   A) General Ledger
   B) Balance Sheet
   C) Income Statement
   D) Cash Flow Statement
   E) Trial Balance

The correct answer is E:) Trial Balance. The trial balance is the starting point for preparing financial statements and when auditors are auditing those statements. It is a compilation of the cumulative ledger totals for all counts that have been debited or credited during the year. This makes it easy to see if any incorrect entries have been made that result in the total debits not being equal to the total credits.

97) Which of the following is NOT true of adjusting entries?

   A) They are typically made on the first day of an accounting period
   B) They typically involve both the balance sheet and the income statement
   C) They can correct the financial statements by more accurately reflecting revenue that has been earned but not recorded
   D) They can correct the financial statements by more accurately reflect expenses that have be incurred but not recorded
   E) All of the above are true

The correct answer is A:) They are typically made on the first day of an accounting period. Adjusting entries are actually made on the last day of the accounting period. Because of the accrual method of accounting it is important that all revenues and expenses are reflected in the proper periods. Adjusting entries allow this by adjusting accounts to most accurately reflect revenues and expenses that occur over time.

98) Where is accrued revenue recorded?

   A) As income on the income statement
   B) As an expense on the income statement
   C) As an asset on the balance sheet
   D) As a liability on the balance sheet
   E) As a contra-revenue account on the balance sheet

The correct answer is C:) As an asset on the balance sheet. Accrued revenue reflects work or services performed that have not yet been billed to a client. The purpose of accrued revenue is to reflect the future benefit of such a transaction in the balance sheet and to match that revenue with expenses incurred in earning it.

99) Which of the following would affect the ending balance in the Cash account?

    A) A sale made for $3,000 which will be paid for on a monthly basis starting next month
    B) An adjusting entry to reflect $2,000 of accrued revenue
    C) The decision to trade a property asset for an equipment asset
    D) A choice to purchase 6 months of pre-paid insurance with cash
    E) None of the above

The correct answer is D:) A choice to purchase 6 months of pre-paid insurance with cash. Although the other options will require entries affecting net income and other asset accounts, only this transaction would result in a change to the cash account for the period.

100) Which of the following would affect the ending balance of liabilities?

    A) Purchasing a new piece of equipment for $1,000 in cash
    B) Taking out a loan to purchase a new piece of property
    C) Selling 1,000 shares of treasury stock and creating an account receivable
    D) Trading one bond for another of equal value
    E) None of the above

The correct answer is B:) Taking out a loan to purchase a new piece of property. In this situation the asset section would increase by the value of the property, and the liability section would increase by the amount of the loan. Each of the other options would affect asset or equity accounts.

Cash		PP&E	
5000		2500	
100	500	500	
1000	600		

Inventory		Notes Payable	
10000			300
	100	600	1000
500			500

101) What is the ending balance in the Cash account?

   A) $4,000 Debit
   B) $5,000 Debit
   C) $5,000 Credit
   D) $7,200 Debit
   E) $7,200 Credit

The correct answer is B:) $5,000 Debit. Cash is an asset account, meaning it will normally have a debit balance. In this case, the account began with a debit balance of $5,000. The subsequent debits for $1,000 and $100 bring the balance to a $6,100. The two credits for $500 and $600 return the balance to a $5,000 debit.

102) What is the ending balance in the PP&E account?

   A) $2,000 Debit
   B) $2,000 Credit
   C) $2,500 Debit
   D) $3,000 Debit
   E) $3,000 Credit

The correct answer is D:) $3,000 Debit. Property, Plant and Equipment (or PP&E) is an asset account and will normally have a debit balance.

103) What is the ending balance in the Notes Payable account?

A) $1,800 Debit
B) $1,800 Credit
C) $1,500 Credit
D) $1,200 Debit
E) $1,200 Credit

The correct answer is E:) $1,200 Credit. Notes Payable is a liability account and will normally have a credit balance. In this case the account starts with $300 as a credit. Credit amounts totaling $1,500 are added to that, and a debit amount of $600 reduces the total. This results in an ending balancing of a $1,200 credit.

104) Which Financial Statement is prepared first?

A) Income Statement
B) Balance Sheet
C) Statement of Cash Flows
D) Statement of Retained Earnings
E) None of the above

The correct answer is A:) Income Statement. The income statement is prepared first because each of the other statements are affected by the calculated net income. The Net Income is used in preparing the statement of retained earnings, and the ending balance of retained earnings affects the equity section of the balance sheet.

105) Corrections for errors in prior years are shown on which statement?

A) Statement of Cash Flows
B) Statement of Retained Earnings
C) Balance Sheet
D) Income Statement
E) None of the above

The correct answer is B:) Statement of Retained Earnings. Because the errors were made in prior years they should not be reflected on the current year's Income Statement or Cash Flow statement. If they were it would make the current year's statement inaccurate. Because Retained Earnings is an accrual account, the adjustments are made there if any previous mistakes are discovered.

106) Which of the following accounts gets closed out at the end of the accounting cycle?

A) Retained Earnings
B) Accumulated Depreciation
C) Property, Plant, and Equipment
D) Unearned Revenue
E) Utilities Expense

The correct answer is E:) Utilities Expense. Accounts on the Income Statement are known as temporary accounts because they reset for each fiscal year. In order to return the accounts to a zero balance the accounts are closed at the end of the cycle. Each of the accounts listed are balance sheet accounts that carry over from year to year except for the utilities expense.

107) Which statement is TRUE of a fiscal year?

A) It must run the same as the calendar year (from January 1 to December 31)
B) It must run based on when taxes are due each year (from April 16 to April 15)
C) It can run over any period that makes the most sense for a particular business
D) It must run either according to the calendar year or the tax year
E) None of the above

The correct answer is C:) It can run over any period that makes the most sense for a particular business. The fiscal year is the reporting period over which financial reports are generated. For example, the U.S. government has a fiscal year that begins each year on October 1.

108) Which statement should be used to determine whether there was a net loss or net profit for a fiscal period?

A) Balance Sheet
B) Income Statement
C) Statement of Cash Flows
D) Statement of Retained Earnings
E) Multiple statements must be used

The correct answer is B:) Income Statement. The Income Statement compiles all revenues and expenses during a period, and totals them to reflect the net profit or loss for that period.

109) Where is Retained Earnings reflected on the Balance Sheet?

    A) Assets
    B) Liabilities
    C) Owner's Equity
    D) Expense
    E) Revenue

The correct answer is C:) Owner's Equity. Retained Earnings reflects the accumulated earnings that are kept within the company over time. This makes it an Equity account.

110) Where is Unearned Revenue reflected on the Balance Sheet?

    A) Assets
    B) Liabilities
    C) Owner's Equity
    D) Expense
    E) Revenue

The correct answer is B:) Liabilities. Unearned Revenue is generated when payment is collected for a service or good that has not been completed. Therefore, the company still holds a liability until the revenue has been technically earned.

111) Where is Accounts Receivable reflected on the Balance Sheet?

    A) Assets
    B) Liabilities
    C) Owner's Equity
    D) Expense
    E) Revenue

The correct answer is A:) Assets. Accounts Receivable is a reflection of an amount that is owed to the company but which hasn't been collected. Once the amount is collected it is moved from the Accounts Receivable account to another asset, such as cash if the payment was made in cash.

112) Which two accounts are affected when depreciation is recorded?

A) Accumulated Depreciation and Depreciation Revenue
B) Depreciation Expense and Account Payable
C) Accumulated Depreciation and Depreciation Expense
D) Depreciation Expense and Property, Plant and Equipment
E) Property, Plant and Equipment and Accumulated Depreciation

The correct answer is C:) Accumulated Depreciation and Depreciation Expense. In this entry Depreciation Expense is the debit and Accumulated Depreciation is the credit. Accumulated Depreciation is then shown as a line item underneath Property, Plant and Equipment so that the present value of the assets can be seen along with their original value.

113) Where is Accumulated Depreciation shown on the financial statements?

A) Assets
B) Liabilities
C) Expenses
D) Revenue
E) Equity

The correct answer is A:) Assets. Accumulated Depreciation is a Contra Asset account. This means that it is reflected in the asset section even though it has a credit balance. It is placed here so that it can offset the value of the items for which the depreciation is being recorded and so that the true value of those items can be clearly seen.

114) ABC Company purchases $10,000 of inventory on account from XYZ Company. How would this be recorded?

A) Debit Inventory for $10,000 and credit Account Receivable for $10,000
B) Debit Inventory for $10,000 and credit Account Payable for $10,000
C) Credit Inventory for $10,000 and debit Account Receivable for $10,000
D) Credit Inventory for $10,000 and debit Account Payable for $10,000
E) Debit Inventory for $10,000 and credit Cost of Goods Sold for $10,000

The correct answer is B:) Debit Inventory for $10,000 and credit Account Payable for $10,000. The debit to inventory will increase the amount of inventory by the amount purchased. However, the company still holds a liability to pay for that inventory, and the liability is reflected by the credit to Account Payable.

115) ABC has a beginning inventory amount of $10,000 and an ending inventory amount of $5,000. Inventory of $2,000 was purchased during the period. Sales for the reporting period are $8,000. What is the gross profit?

A) $1,000
B) $2,000
C) $3,000
D) $5,000
E) $8,000

The correct answer is A:) $1,000. Gross profit is calculated as Sales Revenue-Cost of Goods Sold. For this period, the cost of goods sold can be found by calculating that inventory decreased by a total of $7,000 for the period ($10,000 at the beginning + $2,000 purchased – $5,000 remaining). Therefore, gross profit is $8,000 - $7,000.

116) Based on the following information, which inventory cost method would allow for the highest profits to be recorded?

- 100 units of inventory purchased for $1,000 on January 1
- 50 units of inventory sold for $1,000 on February 14
- 50 units of inventory purchased for $750 on May 1
- 50 units of inventory sold for $1,000 on June 12
- 150 units of inventory purchased for $2,250 on July 1

A) FIFO
B) LIFO
C) Average
D) Either A or C
E) Either A or B

The correct answer is A:) FIFO. Under the FIFO method COGS would be $1,000. Under the LIFO method COGS would be $1,250. Under the average costing method COGS would be $1,125.

117) Given the following entries for a period, determine the total Cost of Goods Sold.

Date	Account		
1-Jan	Inventory	100	
	Cash		100
15-Jan	Cash	200	
	Sales		200
	COGS	100	
	Inventory		100
18-Jan	Inventory	500	
	Account Payable		500
1-Feb	Account Payable	200	
	Cash		200
15-Feb	Account Receivable	300	
	Sales		300
	COGS	150	
	Inventory		150

A) $100
B) $150
C) $250
D) $300
E) $500

The correct answer is C:) $250. Two sales were recorded for the period with total Cost of Goods Sold of $150 and $100. This makes the total Cost of Goods Sold for the period $250.

118) Which cost method will reflect the highest profit margin during times of inflation?

A) LIFO
B) Specific
C) Average
D) FIFO
E) Either A or D

The correct answer is D:) FIFO. Using the FIFO method will result in the lowest Cost of Goods Sold in times of inflation (inventory purchased earlier will have cost less). This will result in the greatest possible profit.

Test-Taking Strategies

Here are some test-taking strategies that are specific to this test and to other CLEP tests in general:

- Keep your eyes on the time. Pay attention to how much time you have left.

- Read the entire question and read all the answers. Many questions are not as hard to answer as they may seem. Sometimes, a difficult sounding question really only is asking you how to read an accompanying chart. Chart and graph questions are on most CLEP tests and should be an easy free point.

- If you don't know the answer immediately, the new computer-based testing lets you mark questions and come back to them later if you have time.

- Read the wording carefully. Some words can give you hints to the right answer. There are no exceptions to an answer when there are words in the question such as always, all or none. If one of the answer choices includes most or some of the right answers, but not all, then that is not the correct answer. Here is an example:

     The primary colors include all of the following:

     A)   Red, Yellow, Blue, Green
     B)   Red, Green, Yellow
     C)   Red, Orange, Yellow
     D)   Red, Yellow, Blue
     E)   None of the above

Although item A includes all the right answers, it also includes an incorrect answer, making it incorrect. If you didn't read it carefully, were in a hurry, or didn't know the material well, you might fall for this.

- Make a guess on a question that you do not know the answer to. There is no penalty for an incorrect answer. Eliminate the answer choices that you know are incorrect. For example, this will let your guess be a 1 in 3 chance instead.

What Your Score Means

Based on your score, you may, or may not, qualify for credit at your specific institution. At University of Phoenix, a score of 50 is passing for full credit. At Utah Valley State College, the score is unpublished, the school will accept credit on a case-by-case basis. Another school, Brigham Young University (BYU) does not accept CLEP credit. To find out what score you need for credit, you need to get that information from your school's website or academic advisor.

You can score between 20 and 80 on any CLEP test. Some exams include percentile ranks. Each correct answer is worth one point. You lose no points for unanswered or incorrect questions.

Test Preparation

How much you need to study depends on your knowledge of a subject area. If you are interested in literature, took it in school, or enjoy reading then your studying and preparation for the literature or humanities test will not need to be as intensive as someone who is new to literature.

This book is much different than the regular CLEP study guides. This book actually teaches you the information that you need to know to pass the test. If you are particularly interested in an area, or feel like you want more information, do a quick search online. There is a lot you'll need to memorize. Almost everything in this book will be on the test. It is important to understand all major theories and concepts listed in the table of contents. It is also very important to know any bolded words.

Don't worry if you do not understand or know a lot about the area. If you study hard, you can complete and pass the test.

To prepare for the test, make a series of goals. Allot a certain amount of time to review the information you have already studied and to learn additional material. Take notes as you study-it will help you learn the material.

Legal Note

FLASHCARDS

This section contains flashcards for you to use to further your understanding of the material and test yourself on important concepts, names or dates. Read the term or question then flip the page over to check the answer on the back. Keep in mind that this information may not be covered in the text of the study guide. Take your time to study the flashcards, you will need to know and understand these concepts to pass the test.

GAAP

SEC

Dr.

Cr.

Balance Sheet

Assets =

Total Equity

Posting

Securities and Exchange
Commission

Generally Accepted
Accounting Principles

Credit

Debit

Liabilities + Shareholder's
Equity

Snapshot of the
investments of a firm and
the financing of those
investments as of a specific
time

Copying the amount from
the journal entries in the
general journal to the
accounts in the general
ledger

Sum of liabilities plus
shareholder's equity

Net Income =

Revenue

Expenses

ROI

ROA

EPS

Amortization

Patent

Measure the net assets (assets less liabilities) that flow into a firm when it sells goods or renders services

Revenue - Expenses

Return on investment

The net assets that a firm consumes in the process of generating revenues

Earnings per share

Return on asset

A right granted by the federal government to exclude others from the benefits of an invention

Gradual recognition of certain expenses associated with intangible assets over a period of several years

Goodwill

Preferred Stock

Common Stock

Stock that has been re-purchased by the corporation is known as what?

Retained Earnings

Market Liquidity

Current Ratio

Acid Test

A share of stock carrying additional rights above and beyond those conferred by common stock

An intangible asset with no liquid value attached

Treasury stock

Are the most usual and commonly held form of stock in a corporation

The ability to quickly buy or sell a particular item without causing a significant movement in the price

Profits that have not been paid to a company's shareholders as dividends

Measures the ability of a company to use its "near cash" or quick assets to immediately extinguish its current liabilities

Comparison of a firm's current assets to its current liabilities

D/E	EBIT
Cash basis of accounting	Accrual basis of accounting
Allocation of prepaid operating costs	Inventory
Acquisition cost basis	Current cost basis

Earnings Before Interest
and Taxes

Debt to equity ratio

Recognizes the revenue
when the firm sells goods
or renders services

A firm recognizes revenues
from selling goods and
services in the period
when it receives cash from
customers

A stock of goods or other
items that a firm owns and
holds for sale or for further
processing as part of ordinary
business operations

A firm acquires assets for
use in operations but does
not completely use them
during the accounting
period when acquired

Values units in inventory at
a current market price

Values units in inventory
at their historical cost until
sold

Replacement cost	**Net realizable value**
Standard cost	**FIFO**
COGS	**LIFO**
Depreciation	**Annual depreciation =**

The amount that a firm would realize as a willing seller in an arms-length transaction with a willing buyer

The amount the firm would have to pay to acquire the item at that time

First in, first out

A predetermined estimate of what items of manufactured inventory should cost

Last in, first out

Cost of goods sold

Cost - estimated salvage/ estimated life in years

Systematically allocates the cost of these assets to the periods of their use

MACRS

Current liabilities

Long-term debt

FCA

SP

CM

Net profit / equity

Gross profit / balance

Obligations that a firm expects to pay or discharge during the normal operating cycle

Modified Accelerated Cost Recovery System

Full Cost Accounting

Obligations having due dates or maturities more than one year after the balance sheet date are long-term debts

Contribution Margin

Selling Price

Return on assets

Return on equity

Made in the USA
Middletown, DE
12 August 2024

58729090R00077